Table of Contents *(cont.)*

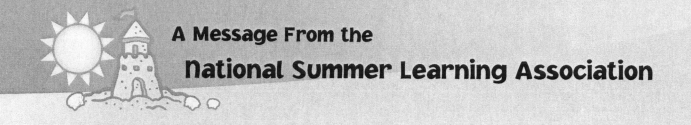

Dear Parents,

Did you know that all young people experience learning losses when they don't engage in educational activities during the summer? That means some of what they've spent time learning over the preceding school year evaporates during the summer months. However, summer learning loss *is* something that you can help prevent. Summer is the perfect time for fun and engaging activities that can help children maintain and grow their academic skills. Here are just a few:

- ✿ Read with your child every day. Visit your local library together, and select books on subjects that interest your child.

- ✿ Ask your child's teacher for recommendations of books for summer reading. The Summer Reading List in this publication is a good start.

- ✿ Explore parks, nature preserves, museums, and cultural centers.

- ✿ Consider every day as a day full of teachable moments. Measuring in recipes and reviewing maps before a car trip are ways to learn or reinforce a skill. Use the Learning Experiences in the back of this book for more ideas.

- ✿ Each day, set goals to accomplish. For example, do five math problems or read a chapter in a book.

- ✿ Encourage your child to complete the activities in books, such as *Summertime Learning*, to help bridge the summer learning gap.

Our vision is for every child to be safe, healthy, and engaged in learning during the summer. Learn more at *www.summerlearning.org* and *www.summerlearningcampaign.org*.

Have a *memorable* summer!

Ron Fairchild
Chief Executive Officer
National Summer Learning Association

Editor
Erica N. Russikoff, M.A.

Contributing Editor
Christine Smith

Illustrators
Mark Mason
Renée Christine Yates

Cover Artist
Tony Carrillo

Editor in Chief
Ina Massler Levin, M.A.

Creative Director
Karen J. Goldfluss, M.S. Ed.

Imaging
Rosa C. See

Publisher

Mary D. Smith, M.S. Ed.

Teacher Created Resources, Inc.
12621 Western Avenue
Garden Grove, CA 92841
www.teachercreated.com
ISBN: 978-1-4206-8841-2

©2010 Teacher Created Resources, Inc.
Reprinted, 2021 (PO603233)
Made in U.S.A.

Table of Contents

How to Use This Book

As a parent, you know that summertime is a time for fun and learning. So it is quite useful that fun and learning can go hand in hand when your child uses *Summertime Learning*.

There are many ways to use this book effectively with your child. We list three ideas on page 6. (See "Day by Day," "Pick and Choose," and "All of a Kind.") You may choose one way on one day, and, on another day, choose something else.

Book Organization

Summertime Learning is organized around an eight-week summer vacation period. For each weekday, there are two lessons. Each Monday through Thursday, there is a math lesson. Additionally, during the odd-numbered weeks, there is a reading lesson on Monday and Wednesday and a writing lesson on Tuesday and Thursday. During the even-numbered weeks, these lessons switch days. (Reading lessons are on Tuesday and Thursday, and writing lessons are on Monday and Wednesday.) Friday features two Friday Fun activities (one typically being a puzzle). The calendar looks like this:

Day	Week 1	Week 2	Week 3	Week 4	Week 5	Week 6	Week 7	Week 8
M	Math ---------- Reading	Math ---------- Writing	Math ---------- Reading	Math ---------- Writing	Math ---------- Reading	Math ---------- Writing	Math ---------- Reading	Math ---------- Writing
T	Math ---------- Writing	Math ---------- Reading	Math ---------- Writing	Math ---------- Reading	Math ---------- Writing	Math ---------- Reading	Math ---------- Writing	Math ---------- Reading
W	Math ---------- Reading	Math ---------- Writing	Math ---------- Reading	Math ---------- Writing	Math ---------- Reading	Math ---------- Writing	Math ---------- Reading	Math ---------- Writing
Th	Math ---------- Writing	Math ---------- Reading	Math ---------- Writing	Math ---------- Reading	Math ---------- Writing	Math ---------- Reading	Math ---------- Writing	Math ---------- Reading
F	Friday Fun ---------- Friday Fun	Friday Fun ---------- Friday Fun	Friday Fun ---------- Friday Fun	Friday Fun ---------- Friday Fun	Friday Fun ---------- Friday Fun	Friday Fun ---------- Friday Fun	Friday Fun ---------- Friday Fun	Friday Fun ---------- Friday Fun

How to Use This Book
(cont.)

Day by Day

You can have your child do the activities in order, beginning on the first Monday of summer vacation. He or she can complete the two lessons provided for each day. It does not matter if math, reading, or writing is completed first. The pages are designed so that each day of the week's lessons are back to back. The book is also perforated. This gives you the option of tearing the pages out for your child to work on. If you opt to have your child tear out the pages, you might want to store the completed pages in a special folder or three-ring binder that your child decorates.

Pick and Choose

You may find that you do not want to have your child work strictly in order. Feel free to pick and choose any combination of pages based on your child's needs and interests.

All of a Kind

Perhaps your child needs more help in one area than another. You may opt to have him or her work only on math, reading, or writing.

Keeping Track

A Reward Chart is included on page 10 of this book, so you and your child can keep track of the activities that have been completed. This page is designed to be used with the stickers provided. Once your child has finished a page, have him or her put a sticker on the castle. If you don't want to use stickers for this, have your child color in a circle each time an activity is completed.

The stickers can also be used on the individual pages. As your child finishes a page, let him or her place a sticker in the sun at the top of the page. If he or she asks where to begin the next day, simply have him or her start on the page after the last sticker.

There are enough stickers to use for both the Reward Chart and the sun on each page. Plus, there are extra stickers for your child to enjoy.

Standards and Skills

Each activity in *Summertime Learning* meets one or more of the following standards and skills*. Visit *http://www.teachercreated.com/standards/* for correlations to the Common Core State Standards. The activities in this book are designed to help your child reinforce the skills learned during kindergarten, as well as introduce new skills that will be learned in first grade.

Language Arts Standards
- Uses the general skills and strategies of the writing process
- Uses the stylistic and rhetorical aspects of writing
- Uses grammatical and mechanical conventions in written compositions
- Gathers and uses information for research purposes
- Uses the general skills and strategies of the reading process
- Uses reading skills and strategies to understand and interpret a variety of literary texts
- Uses reading skills and strategies to understand and interpret a variety of informational texts
- Uses listening and speaking strategies for different purposes
- Uses viewing skills and strategies to understand and interpret visual media
- Understands the characteristics and components of the media

Mathematics Standards
- Uses a variety of strategies in the problem-solving process
- Understands and applies basic and advanced properties of the concepts of numbers
- Uses basic and advanced procedures while performing the processes of computation
- Understands and applies basic and advanced properties of the concepts of measurement
- Understands and applies basic and advanced properties of the concepts of geometry
- Understands and applies basic and advanced concepts of statistics and data analysis
- Understands and applies basic and advanced concepts of probability
- Understands and applies basic and advanced properties of functions and algebra

Writing Skills
- Uses prewriting strategies to plan written work
- Revises and edits written work by adding descriptive words and details; rearranging words and sentences to clarify meaning; and checking punctuation, capitalization, and spelling
- Uses legible handwriting and/or a computer to publish work
- Incorporates illustrations or photos
- Organizes written work
- Writes in a variety of forms or genres
- Writes for different purposes
- Uses descriptive words to express ideas
- Uses declarative and interrogative sentences in written compositions
- Uses upper- and lowercase letters of the alphabet, spaces words and sentences, writes from left-to-right and top-to-bottom, includes margins
- Uses complete sentences in written compositions
- Uses nouns, verbs, adjectives, and adverbs

Standards and Skills
(cont.)

Writing Skills *(cont.)*
- Uses conventions of spelling in written compositions
- Knows to capitalize names and the first words of sentences
- Uses periods after declarative sentences and question marks after interrogative sentences

Reading Skills
- Uses mental images based on pictures and print to aid in comprehension of text
- Uses meaning clues to aid comprehension and make predictions about content
- Uses basic elements of phonetic analysis to decode unknown words
- Understands level-appropriate sight words and vocabulary
- Reads familiar stories, poems, and passages aloud with fluency and expression
- Understands a variety of literary passages and texts
- Uses reading skills and strategies to understand informational texts
- Can retell a fictional or informational text in own words

Mathematics Skills
- Draws pictures to represent problems
- Can explain how she or he solved a numerical problem
- Makes organized lists or tables of information necessary for solving a problem
- Uses pattern blocks, tiles, or other manipulative materials to represent problems
- Understands that numbers represent quantities of objects
- Counts whole numbers
- Understands symbolic, concrete, and pictorial representations of numbers
- Understands the basic whole-number relationships of "less than" and "greater than"
- Understands the concept of a unit and its division into equal parts
- Adds and subtracts whole numbers
- Can determine whether to use addition or subtraction to solve a problem
- Understands the basic measurements of length, width, height, weight, and temperature
- Understands the concept of time and how it is measured
- Knows how to tell time and measure length, weight, and temperature
- Can estimate familiar linear dimensions, weights, and time intervals
- Understands basic properties of (e.g., number of sides, corners, square corners) and similarities and differences between simple geometric shapes
- Can identify left and right
- Understands that patterns can be made by putting different shapes together or taking them apart
- Understands the basic concept of a graph and that information can be represented in graphs
- Collects and represents information about objects or events in simple graphs
- Extends simple patterns

* Standards and skills used with permission from McREL (Copyright 2009, McREL. Mid-continent Research for Education and Learning. Address: 4601 DTC Boulevard, Suite 500, Denver, CO 80237. Telephone: 303-337-0990. Web site: www.mcrel.org/standards-benchmarks)

More Friday Fun

The Friday Fun activities in this book are an entertaining way to wrap up a week of learning while still providing your child with enrichment in a variety of areas. In addition to the written activities provided, consider incorporating the following interactive games and activities to extend your child's learning beyond the page.

Week 1: What Comes Next?

Go on a pattern hunt with your child at home, in your neighborhood, or at a shopping mall. Look for patterns in clothing, tiles, furniture, etc. Then, let your child make his or her own patterns using beads, stickers, or rubber stamps. Ask your child to explain the patterns to you.

Week 2: What Covers Me?

Visit a zoo or large pet store with your child. Have your child make a list of the animals he or she sees. After returning home, help your child put the animals in groups by type of body covering, the food they eat, where they live, etc. Talk about the different groups with your child. Which group has the most? Which group has the least?

Week 3: Create a Clown

Make a set of shapes, including circles, ovals, triangles, rectangles, and squares of different sizes, out of construction paper. Challenge your child to make a picture of something using some of the shapes. Have your child write about his or her creation. What is it? What does it do?

Week 4: Finish Line

Head outside with family and friends for some exercise, fun, and friendly competition. Arrange to have several races such as running, crab-walking, and hopping. Award ribbons or medals for first, second, and third place.

Week 5: Barnyard Animals

Play "Farmer Brown Says." Say "Farmer Brown says . . ." followed by an action that specifies left or right. (Example: "Farmer Brown says touch your left ear.") Your child should only do what Farmer Brown says, so occasionally give a direction without saying "Farmer Brown says." If your child does something that Farmer Brown does not tell him or her to do, he or she is out. Play several times, and take turns being Farmer Brown.

Week 6: The Right Tool

Set up a measuring area to give your child an opportunity to use measuring tools. You could include a stopwatch, a cooking timer, a ruler, a tape measure, dry and liquid measuring cups, a scale, and things to measure (such as fruit, small toys, water, etc.).

Week 7: Draw It

Visit an art museum with your child, and talk about the different pieces you see. How are they similar? How are they different? Which ones do you like or dislike and why? After your visit, create your own sidewalk art exhibit using sidewalk chalk. Be sure to take photographs of your masterpieces to preserve them.

Week 8: What's for Dinner?

Work with your child to plan a nutritious meal for the family. Talk about the different food groups, and be sure to include foods from the different groups in the meal. Let your child help plan the menu, make the shopping list, do the shopping, and prepare the meal.

Reward Chart

10

©Teacher Created Resources, Inc.

Count, Write, Name

Directions: Count the number of pictures. Write the numeral. Then, write the number name. Use the Word Bank to help you with spelling the number names.

Word Bank

one	three	five	seven
two	four	six	eight

1.

Numeral

Number Name

5.

Numeral

Number Name

2.

Numeral

Number Name

6.

Numeral

Number Name

3.

Numeral

Number Name

7.

Numeral

Number Name

4.

Numeral

Number Name

8.

Numeral

Number Name

Words in a Family

Directions: Say the name of each picture. Write the beginning sound. Then, read all the words in each word family aloud.

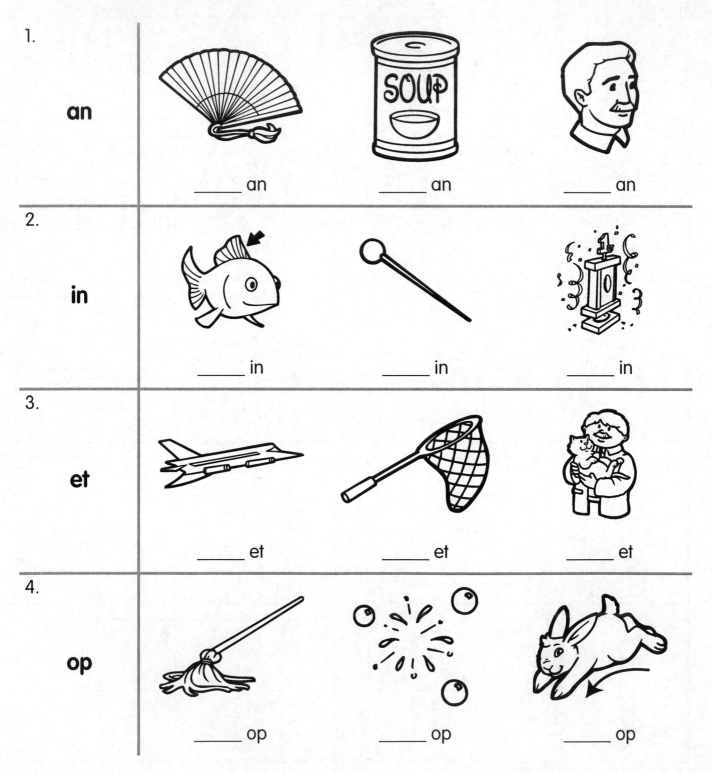

1.

an

_____ an

_____ an

_____ an

2.

in

_____ in

_____ in

_____ in

3.

et

_____ et

_____ et

_____ et

4.

op

_____ op

_____ op

_____ op

Counting Clothes

Directions: Count how many objects are in each set. Write the number in the box.

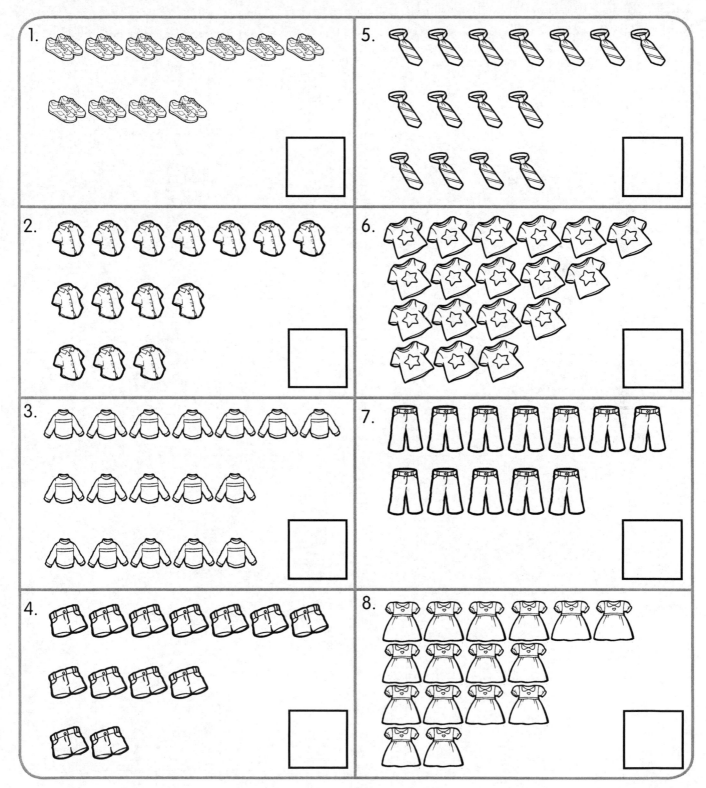

Describe It

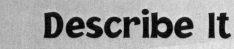

Directions: Write a word that describes each picture below. Use the words in the Word Bank to help you.

Word Bank			
beautiful	cute	quiet	smelly
big	hot	round	three

1. _____

2. _____

3. _____

4. _____

5. _____

6. _____

7. _____

8. _____

Showing Addition

Directions: Write a number sentence to go with set of each pictures.

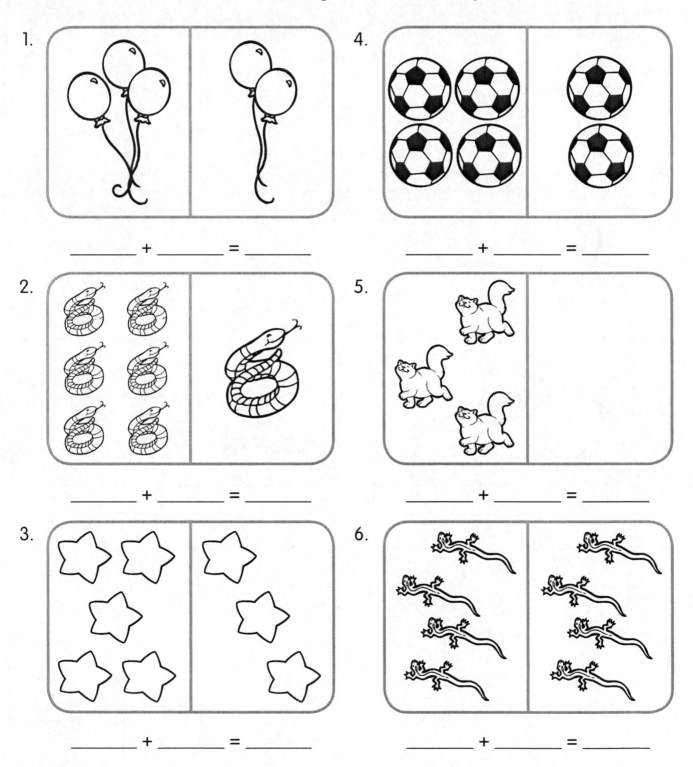

1. _____ + _____ = _____

2. _____ + _____ = _____

3. _____ + _____ = _____

4. _____ + _____ = _____

5. _____ + _____ = _____

6. _____ + _____ = _____

Missing Letters

Directions: Look at the pictures. Say the words. Then, write the missing letters in order to spell the words.

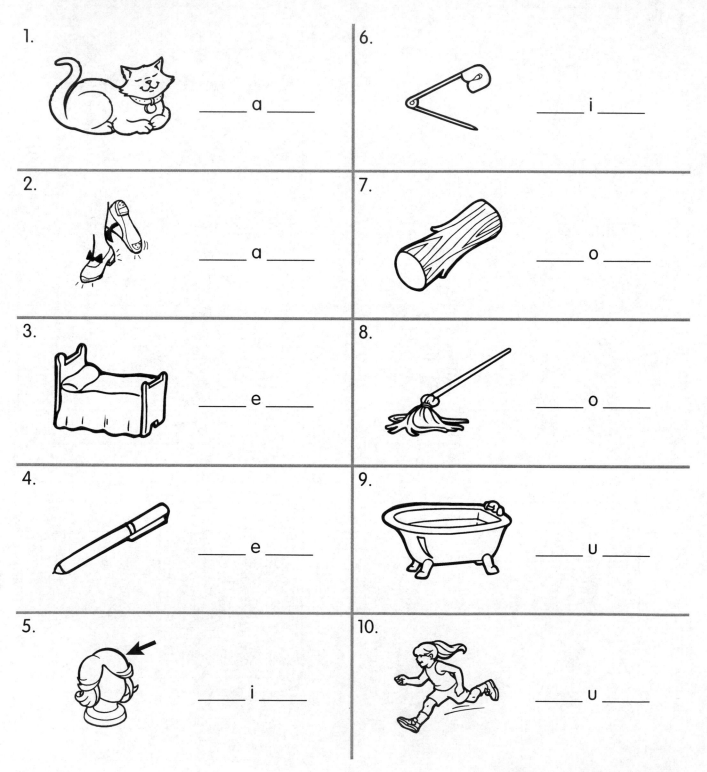

1. ___ a ___

2. ___ a ___

3. ___ e ___

4. ___ e ___

5. ___ i ___

6. ___ i ___

7. ___ o ___

8. ___ o ___

9. ___ u ___

10. ___ u ___

Count the Animals

Directions: Uncle Ted's animals got loose all over the barnyard, and he forgot how many animals he has. Fill in the graph below to help him count his animals.

	1	2	3	4	5	6
pigs						
cows						
sheep						
chickens						
dogs						

1. What animal does he have the most of?_____

2. How many more sheep does he have than dogs? _____

3. How many animals does Uncle Ted have in all? _____

Who I Am

A **complete sentence** is a complete thought with a subject, a verb, and a punctuation mark at the end.

Directions: Write a complete sentence to answer each question below.

✿ What is your name?

_____

✿ When is your birthday?

_____

✿ What is your favorite color?

_____

✿ How old are you?

_____

✿ What is your favorite food?

_____

✿ Do you have any brothers or sisters?

_____

Penguin Poems

Directions: Read the penguin poetry below. Fill in the missing words. Then, try writing some rhymes of your own on a separate sheet of paper.

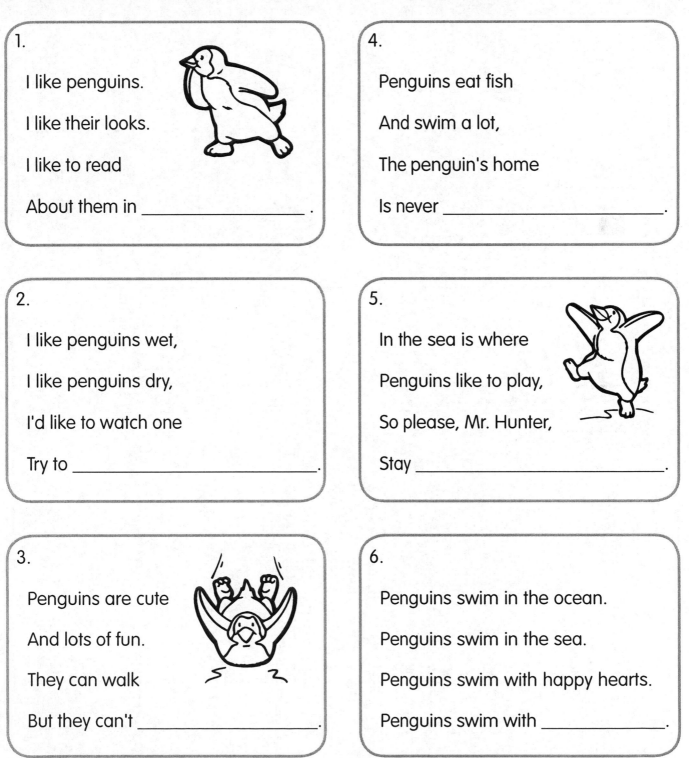

1.

I like penguins.

I like their looks.

I like to read

About them in _____ .

4.

Penguins eat fish

And swim a lot,

The penguin's home

Is never _____ .

2.

I like penguins wet,

I like penguins dry,

I'd like to watch one

Try to _____ .

5.

In the sea is where

Penguins like to play,

So please, Mr. Hunter,

Stay _____ .

3.

Penguins are cute

And lots of fun.

They can walk

But they can't _____ .

6.

Penguins swim in the ocean.

Penguins swim in the sea.

Penguins swim with happy hearts.

Penguins swim with _____ .

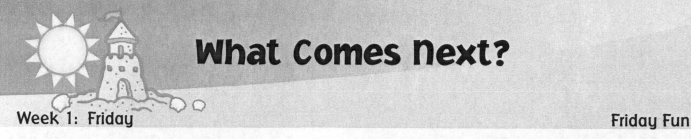

What Comes Next?

Directions: Look at the patterns below. Complete the patterns by drawing what would come next in the box.

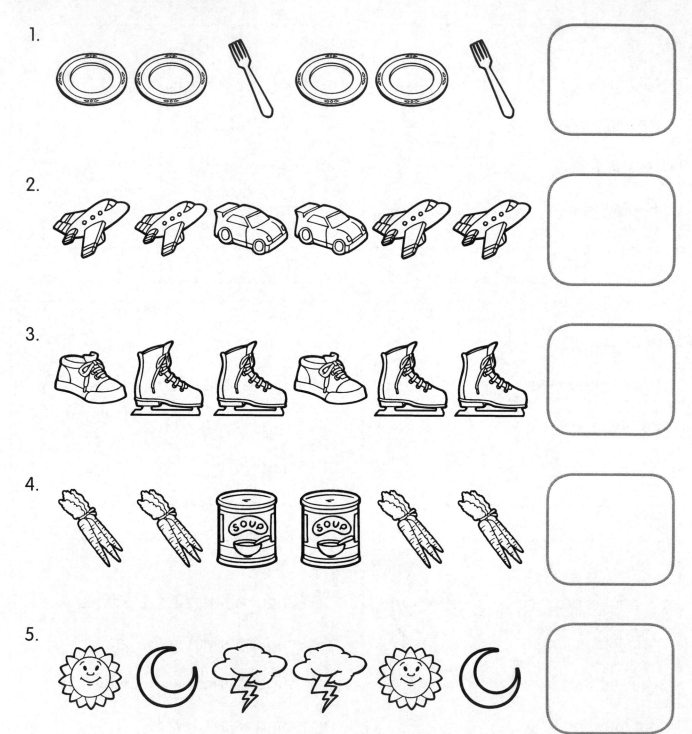

1.

2.

3.

4.

5.

20

©Teacher Created Resources, Inc.

Take It Away

Directions: How many dinosaurs do you need to take away so that the number remaining matches the number on the right? Count backward, and cross out one dinosaur at a time until you reach the right number. Then, write the number of dinosaurs you have crossed out in the square.

1.

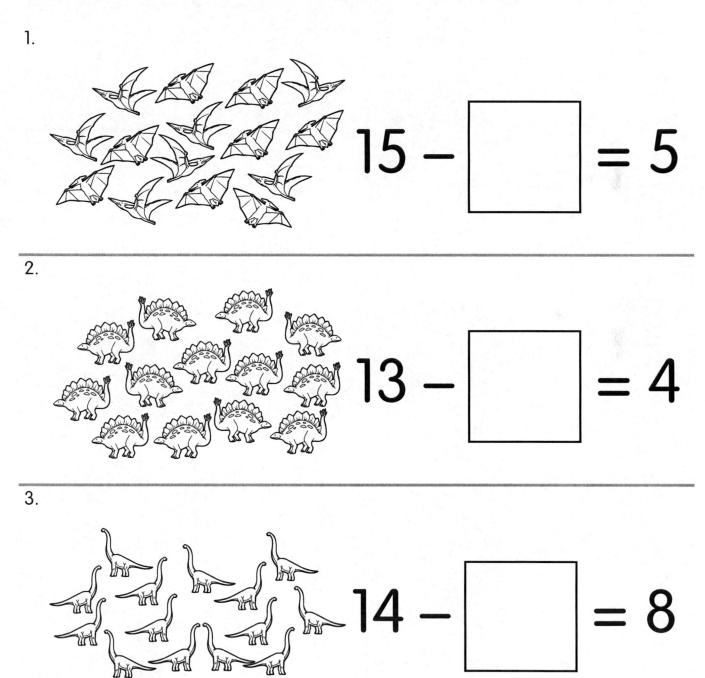

$$15 - \boxed{} = 5$$

2.

$$13 - \boxed{} = 4$$

3.

$$14 - \boxed{} = 8$$

Action Words

Directions: Write the word from each sentence that shows what someone or something does or did.

1. The dog chased the cat.   _____

2. The stars twinkle in the sky.   _____

3. The children watched the parade.   _____

4. My brother set the table.   _____

5. I swim like a fish.   _____

6. The bird sings a pretty song.   _____

7. You eat the last piece.   _____

8. The player threw the ball.   _____

Groups of Two

Math

Directions: Draw the missing pictures in each group. Then, count in groups of two to find out how many there are altogether. Write this number in the circle.

☼ Draw 2 toppings on each pizza.

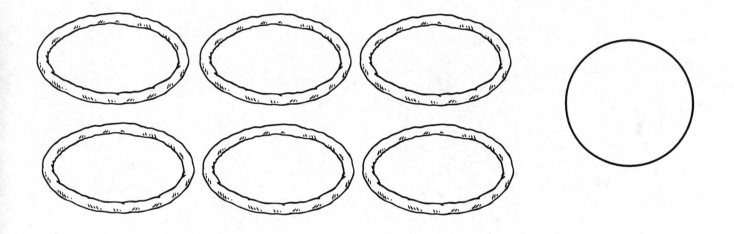

☼ Draw 2 ice cubes in each glass.

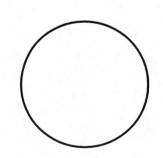

Middle Sounds

Directions: Say the name of each picture. Write the letter of its middle sound.

1.

f _____ n   f _____ n

2.

p _____ n   p _____ n

3.

n _____ t   n _____ t

4.

l _____ g   l _____ g

5.

c _____ t   c _____ t

6.

m _____ p   m _____ p

7.

d _____ g   d _____ g

8.

b _____ g   b _____ g

Shade the Shapes

Directions: Color part of each shape as follows: $\frac{1}{2}$ = brown, $\frac{1}{3}$ = yellow, $\frac{1}{4}$ = red.

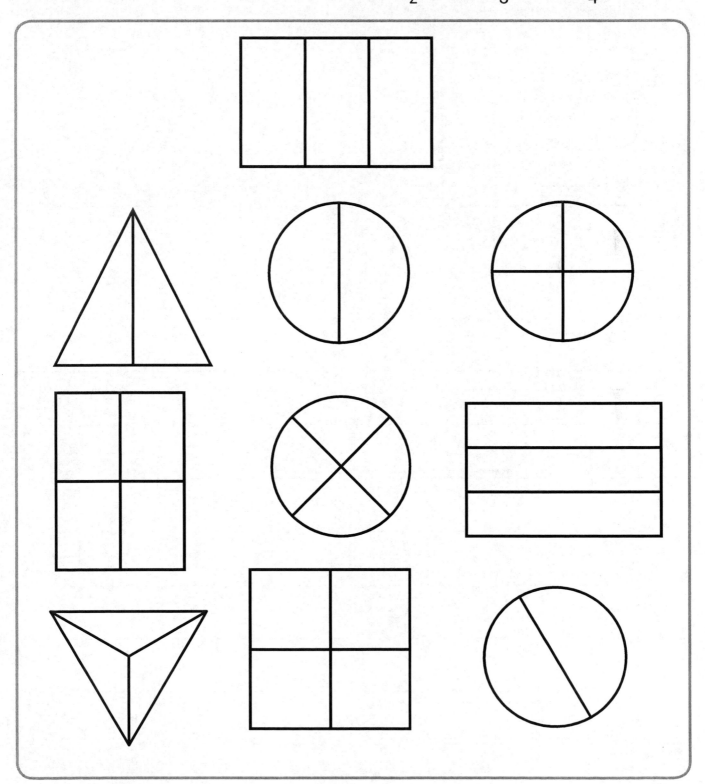

Get It Together

Directions: Look at the parts of the story below. All the parts are mixed up. Write the story in the correct order on the lines below.

Then, I looked under the table.
There was my cat sitting in the closet!
Finally, I looked in the closet.
First, I looked under my bed.
This morning, my cat got lost.
The Lost Cat

_____

_____

_____

_____

_____

_____

_____

_____

Leap Frog

Directions: Imagine you are a frog. You can jump forward on a number line to help you add. Start at 0 and jump all the way to the first number. Then, count on to match the second number by making small jumps. The number you land on is your answer. The first one has been started for you.

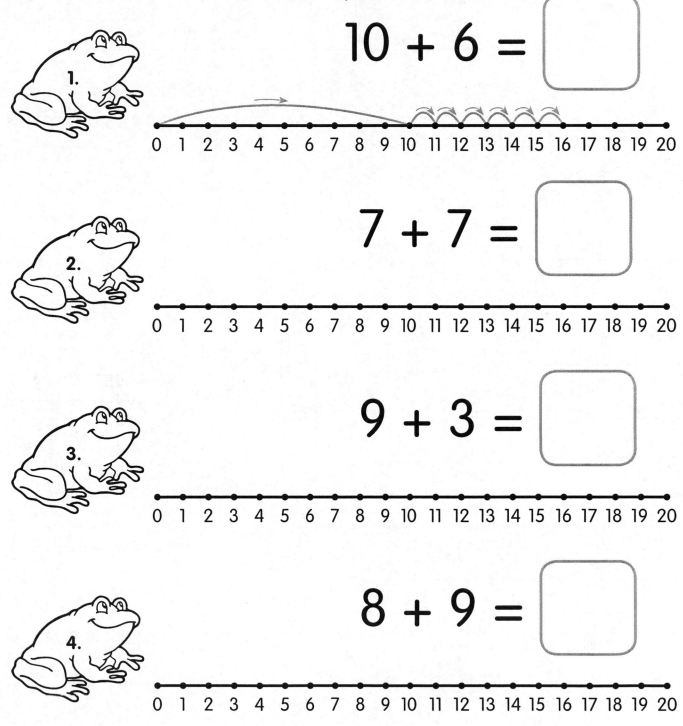

1.
$$10 + 6 = \boxed{}$$

0 1 2 3 4 5 6 7 8 9 10 11 12 13 14 15 16 17 18 19 20

2.
$$7 + 7 = \boxed{}$$

0 1 2 3 4 5 6 7 8 9 10 11 12 13 14 15 16 17 18 19 20

3.
$$9 + 3 = \boxed{}$$

0 1 2 3 4 5 6 7 8 9 10 11 12 13 14 15 16 17 18 19 20

4.
$$8 + 9 = \boxed{}$$

0 1 2 3 4 5 6 7 8 9 10 11 12 13 14 15 16 17 18 19 20

Missing Words

Directions: What word is missing from each set of words? Write it on the lines.

1. _____ Bo Peep

   _____ Boy Blue

   _____ Red Riding Hood

2. The _____ Little Pigs

   The _____ Bears

   The _____ Billy Goats Gruff

3. Rock-a-bye _____

   Bye, Bye _____ Bunting

   Hush, Little _____

4. _____ Mother Hubbard

   This _____ Man

   The _____ Woman in the Shoe

It Belongs

Directions: Color the items in each group that belong together. Put an **X** on the item that does not belong.

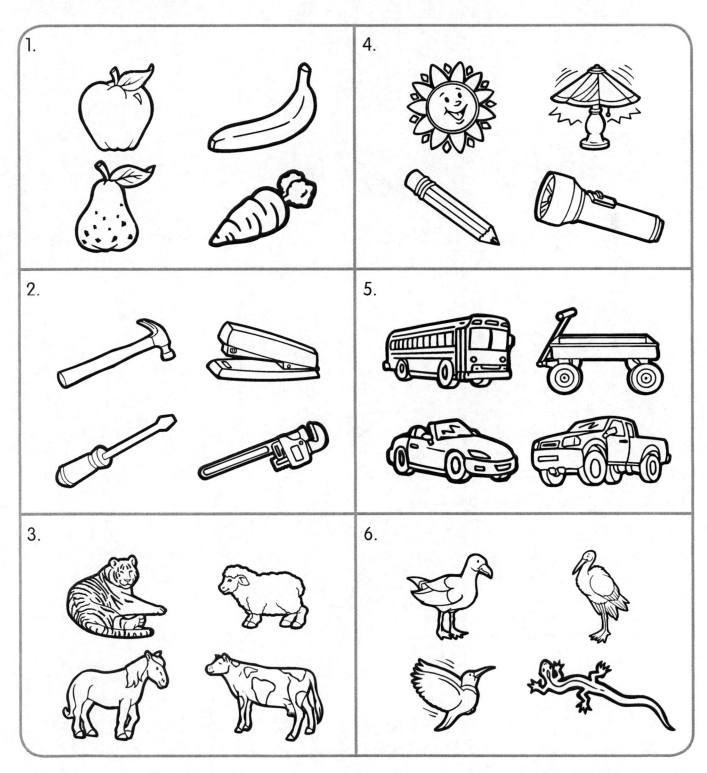

What Covers Me?

Directions: Look at the pictures of the animals below. Circle the type of body covering each animal has. Color the animals with hair. These animals are mammals.

1. feathers   scales

2. feathers   hair

3. feathers   scales

4. hair   scales

5. feathers   hair

6. feathers   scales

7. feathers   scales

8. feathers   hair

9. feathers   scales

Telling Time

Directions: Look at the number the small hand (hour hand) is pointing to on each clock. Circle the number. Then, write that number on the line below each clock to tell the time.

1.

_____ o' clock

2.

_____ o' clock

3.

_____ o' clock

4.

_____ o' clock

5.

_____ o' clock

6.

_____ o' clock

Yes or No?

Directions: Read each sentence. Circle **yes** if it is true. Circle **no** if it is not true.

1. You can pet a cat. yes no	6. A bus has a hand. yes no
2. A hen has a fin. yes no	7. Men can get in a cab. yes no
3. A key can fit in a pot. yes no	8. A kid can get in a bathtub. yes no
4. A jet can dig. yes no	9. A hog can mop. yes no
5. A pen can jog. yes no	10. You put jam on a rug. yes no

Showing Subtraction

Directions: Write a number sentence to go with each picture.

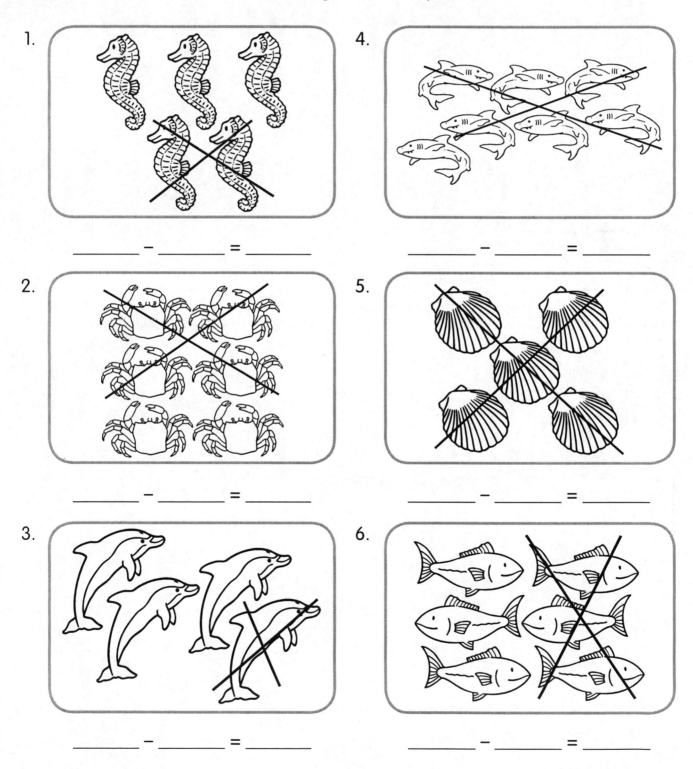

1.

_____ – _____ = _____

2.

_____ – _____ = _____

3.

_____ – _____ = _____

4.

_____ – _____ = _____

5.

_____ – _____ = _____

6.

_____ – _____ = _____

First Words

Directions: Practice capitalizing the first word in each sentence by writing it on the line.

1. _____ mom took me shopping.
   my

2. _____ we play now?
   can

3. _____ like to eat pizza.
   i

4. _____ are going to the movies.
   we

5. _____ helped me bake a cake.
   she

6. _____ are eggs in the nest.
   there

7. _____ you coming with us?
   are

8. _____ favorite color is yellow.
   her

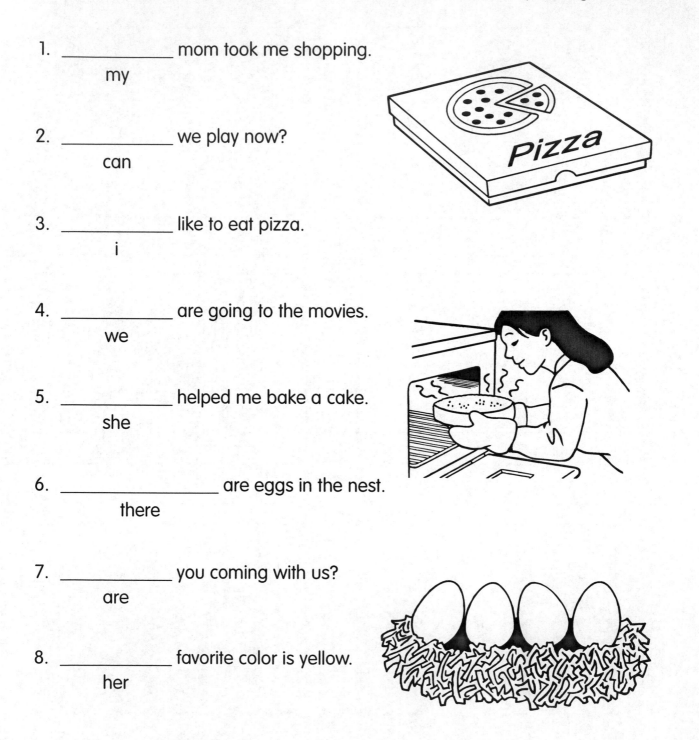

Tick-Tock Clock

Directions: Read the digital time shown below each clock. Then, draw an hour hand and a minute hand on each clock to show the same time.

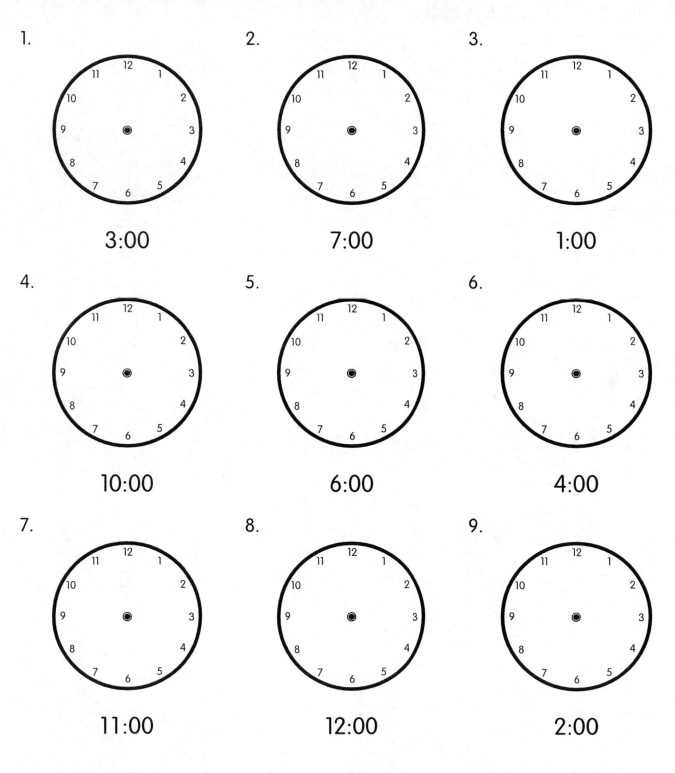

1.

3:00

2.

7:00

3.

1:00

4.

10:00

5.

6:00

6.

4:00

7.

11:00

8.

12:00

9.

2:00

Two Meanings

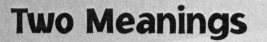

Directions: Look at each pair of pictures. Write a word that names both pictures. Use the words from the Word Bank to help you.

Word Bank

bat   bowl   orange   pot   saw

1. _____

2. _____

3. _____

4. _____

5. _____

Counting the Days

Directions: Use the Days of the Week chart to help you answer the questions below.

Days of the Week

Sunday   Monday   Tuesday   Wednesday   Thursday   Friday   Saturday

1. Today is Thursday. Kyle's party is in three days. What day is the party on?

   _____

2. Yesterday was Sunday. Tomorrow will be Tuesday. What day is it today?

   _____

3. The circus is on Friday. Today is Tuesday. How many days until the circus?

   _____

4. Today is Wednesday. Allison went to karate yesterday, and she will go again tomorrow. What days does Allison go to karate?

   _____

5. Brady has soccer practice on Tuesday. His game is four days later. What day is his game?

   _____

Buggy Sentences

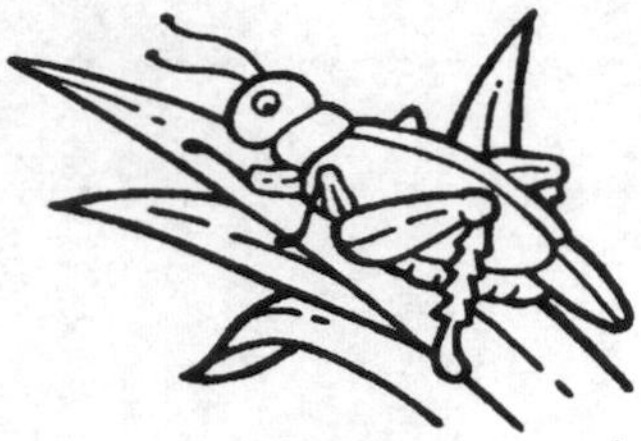

cricket

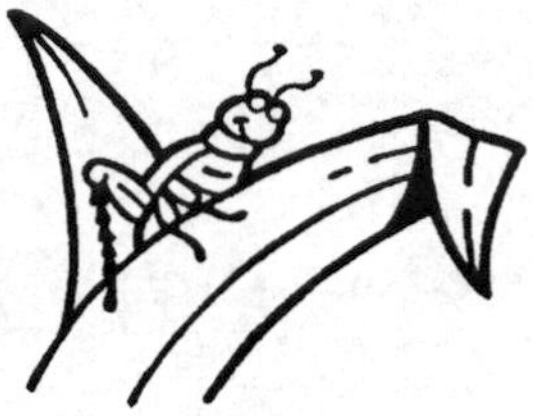

small

hop

chirp

flower

leaf

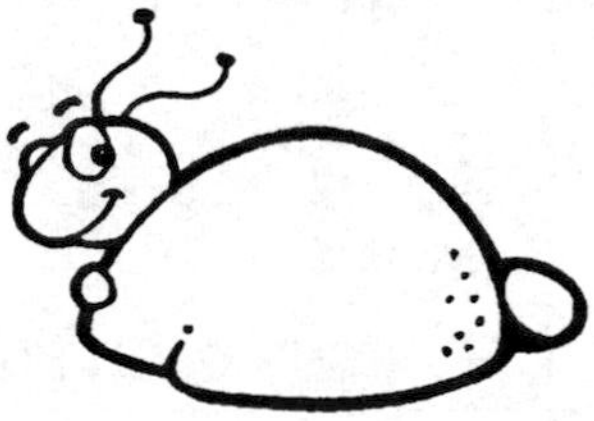

hide

Directions: Create your own sentences using the words above.

1. The cricket is _____ .

2. The cricket _____ .

3. The _____ .

4. _____ .

Opposites

Directions: List the opposites for the words below.

1. hot _____

2. dark _____

3. off _____

4. over _____

5. high _____

6. in _____

7. far _____

8. curly _____

9. up _____

10. happy _____

11. clean _____

12. tall _____

Create a Clown

Directions: Follow the directions below to draw a picture of a clown.

1. Draw a circle for the head.

2. Draw an oval below the circle for the body.

3. Draw a triangle above the head for the hat.

4. Draw two vertical rectangles below the oval for the legs.

5. Draw two horizontal rectangles, one on the left and one on the right side of the oval, for the arms.

6. Draw hands, shoes, and a face. Add other details to the clown picture, such as balloons.

Add Them Up

Directions: Solve the problems.

1. Cheryl has 5 marbles. Cindy has 2 more marbles than Cheryl. How many marbles does Cindy have?

2. Henry has 4 stamps. Eric has 5 more stamps than Henry. How many stamps does Eric have?

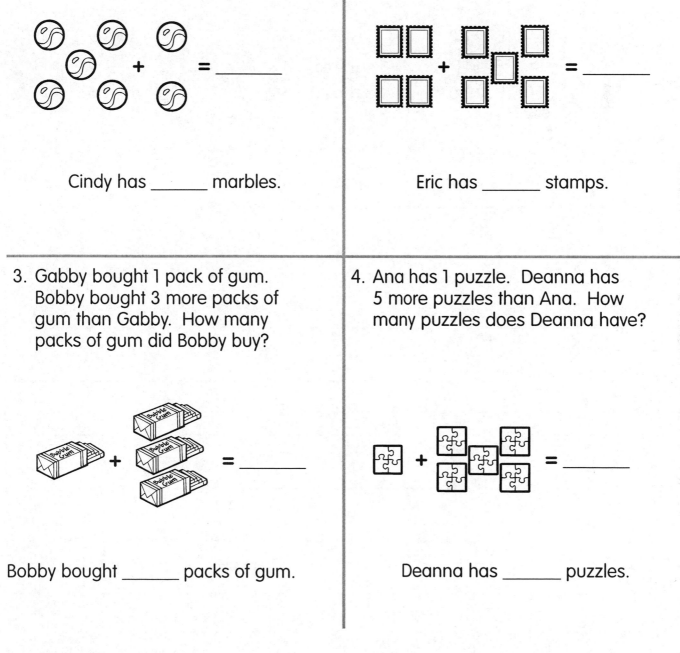

Cindy has _____ marbles.

Eric has _____ stamps.

3. Gabby bought 1 pack of gum. Bobby bought 3 more packs of gum than Gabby. How many packs of gum did Bobby buy?

4. Ana has 1 puzzle. Deanna has 5 more puzzles than Ana. How many puzzles does Deanna have?

Bobby bought _____ packs of gum.

Deanna has _____ puzzles.

Match the Groups

A **complete sentence** is a complete thought with a subject, a verb, and a punctuation mark at the end.

Directions: Match the groups of words to make sentences. Then, write the sentences on the lines below.

1.	The snake	moos.
2.	The rabbit	buzzes.
3.	The lion	chirps.
4.	The dog	jumps.
5.	The bee	barks.
6.	The bird	slithers.
7.	The cow	roars.

1. _____

2. _____

3. _____

4. _____

5. _____

6. _____

7. _____

©*Teacher Created Resources, Inc.*

Missing Numbers

Directions: Help Lindsey and Phil get home. Write the missing numbers from 0 to 100.

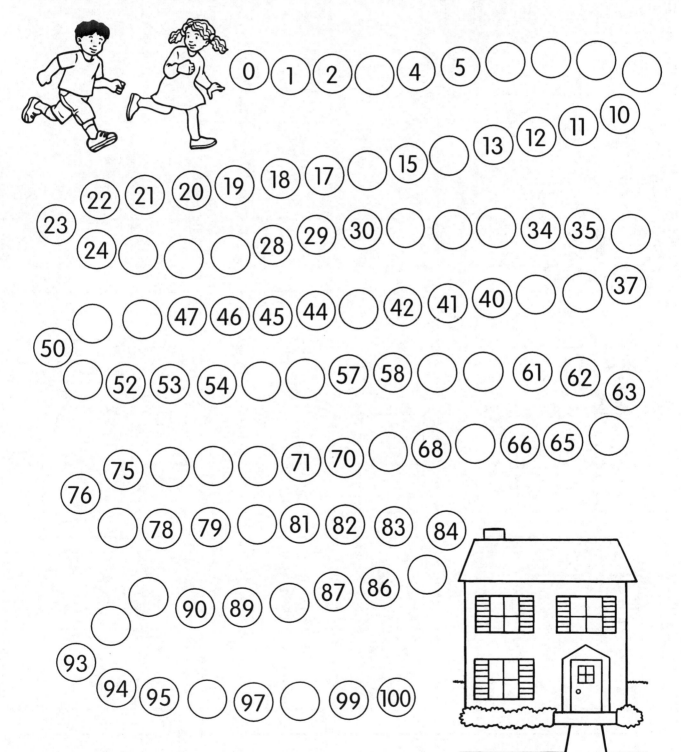

Name the Vowel

Directions: Say the name of each picture. Color the box with the letter that matches the short vowel sound.

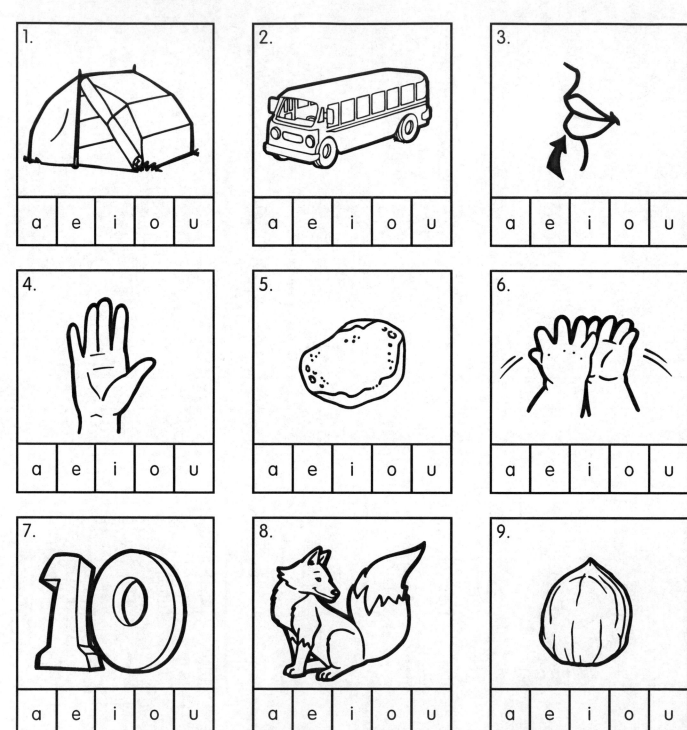

1.

| a | e | i | o | u |

2.

| a | e | i | o | u |

3.

| a | e | i | o | u |

4.

| a | e | i | o | u |

5.

| a | e | i | o | u |

6.

| a | e | i | o | u |

7.

| a | e | i | o | u |

8.

| a | e | i | o | u |

9.

| a | e | i | o | u |

Subtract Them

Directions: Solve the problems.

1. There are 8 chicks. If 2 run away, how many would be left?

There would be _____ chicks left.

2. There are 10 owls. If 9 fly away, how many would be left?

There would be _____ owl left.

3. Noel saw 9 bats sleeping in the hay loft. If 3 of them wake up, how many bats would still be sleeping?

There would still be _____ bats sleeping.

4. Tim has 9 ducks. If 2 ducks waddle away, how many ducks would Tim have left?

Tim would have _____ ducks left.

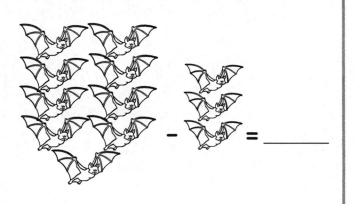

When I Grow Up

Directions: Write about what you will do when you grow up. Draw a picture to match your writing.

_____

_____

_____

_____

Shape Riddles

Directions: Use the shapes to solve the riddles.

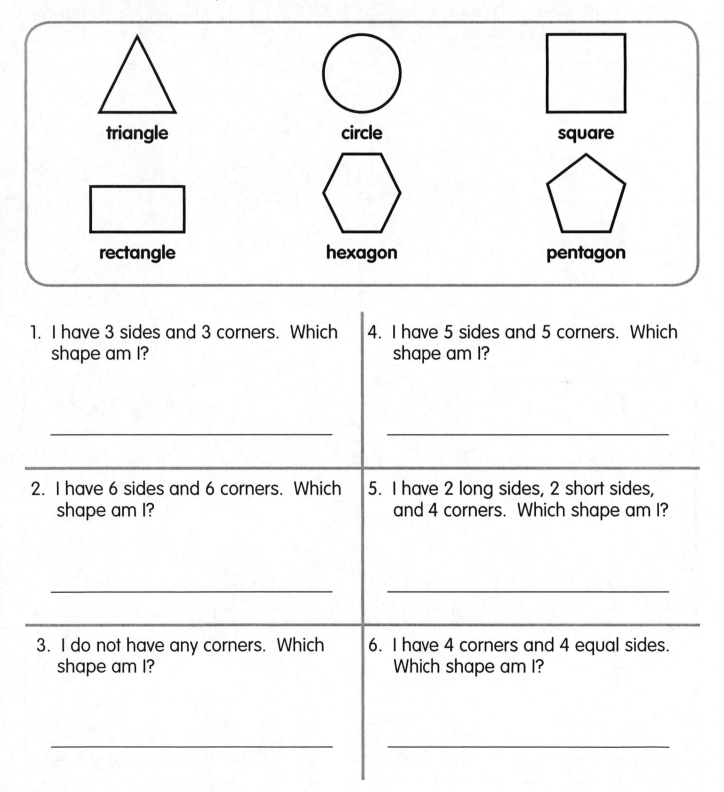

triangle   circle   square

rectangle   hexagon   pentagon

1. I have 3 sides and 3 corners. Which shape am I?

_____

2. I have 6 sides and 6 corners. Which shape am I?

_____

3. I do not have any corners. Which shape am I?

_____

4. I have 5 sides and 5 corners. Which shape am I?

_____

5. I have 2 long sides, 2 short sides, and 4 corners. Which shape am I?

_____

6. I have 4 corners and 4 equal sides. Which shape am I?

_____

Short or Long?

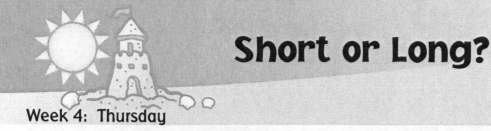

Directions: Say the name of each picture. Print the vowel sound that you hear on the line. If the vowel is **short**, fill in the bubble labeled **short**. If the vowel is **long**, fill in the bubble labeled **long**.

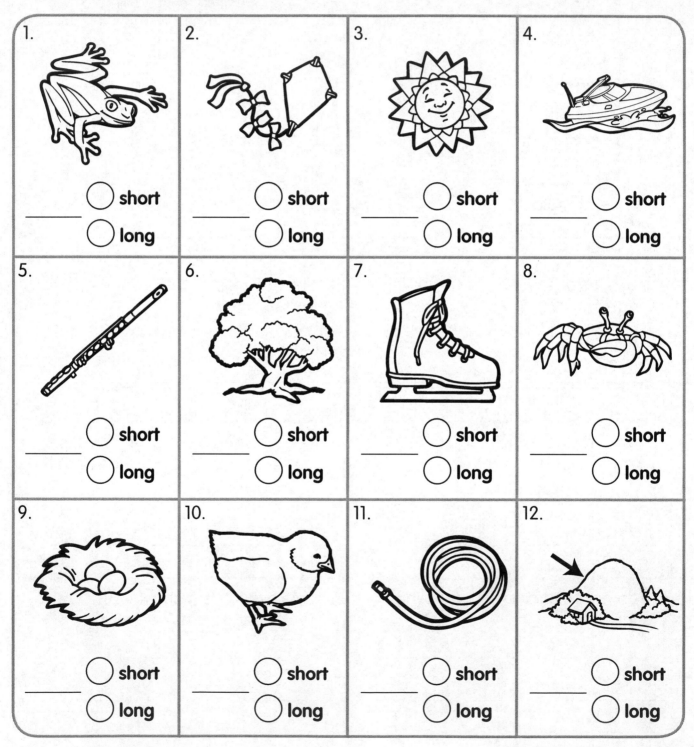

1. ○ short ○ long
2. ○ short ○ long
3. ○ short ○ long
4. ○ short ○ long
5. ○ short ○ long
6. ○ short ○ long
7. ○ short ○ long
8. ○ short ○ long
9. ○ short ○ long
10. ○ short ○ long
11. ○ short ○ long
12. ○ short ○ long

©Teacher Created Resources, Inc.

To the Movies

Directions: Sally, Sam, Sarah, and Sandy went to the movies. Who is first in line? Who is second, third, and last? Use the clues below to help you.

Clues

☼ The first person in line is a boy.

☼ Sarah is holding a bag of popcorn.

☼ Sandy is between Sam and Sally.

☼ Sally is wearing shorts.

Who's **first**? _____

Who's **third**? _____

Who's **second**? _____

Who's **last**? _____

Finish Line

Directions: Color the cars. Then, write the color of the car to show the place in which each will finish the race.

```
Finish

red          orange          yellow

green          blue
```

1. First _____

2. Third _____

3. Fifth _____

4. Second _____

5. Last _____

6. Fourth _____

---

7. What color is the car before the green car? _____

8. What color is the car after the blue car? _____

9. What color is the car after the red car? _____

10. What color is the car before the yellow car? _____

Blast Off!

Directions: Solve each problem. Then, color the puzzle.

> **5** = blue   **6** = red   **7** = gray   **8** = yellow

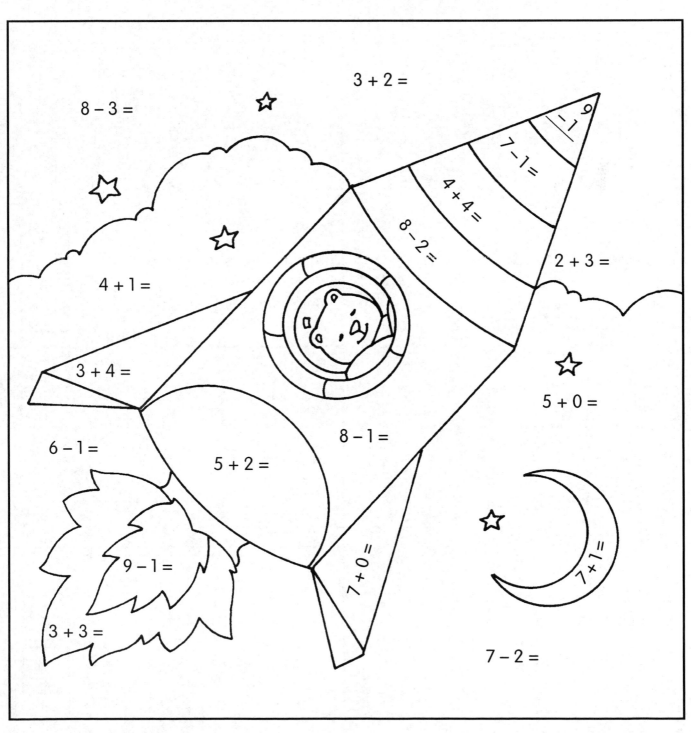

$3 + 2 =$

$8 - 3 =$

$7 - 1 =$

$9 - 1$

$4 + 4 =$

$8 - 2 =$

$2 + 3 =$

$4 + 1 =$

$3 + 4 =$

$8 - 1 =$

$5 + 0 =$

$6 - 1 =$

$5 + 2 =$

$9 - 1 =$

$7 + 0 =$

$7 + 1 =$

$3 + 3 =$

$7 - 2 =$

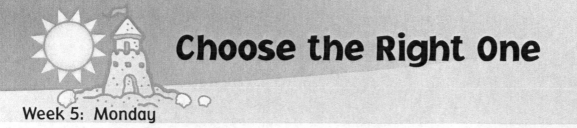

Choose the Right One

Directions: Look at each picture. Then, read the sentences underneath it. Which sentence matches the picture? Put a check in the box next to the correct sentence.

1.

The spider sees a fly. ☐

The spider has one eye. ☐

2.

The rats taint a picture. ☐

The rats paint a picture. ☐

3.

The kid spits beads. ☐

The kid spits seeds. ☐

4.

The pets stomp on ants. ☐

The pets wear pants. ☐

Groups of Ten

Directions: Count how many bees there are below. Write this number at the top. Then, draw a line around each group of 10 bees. The first one has been done for you. How many groups have you made? Write this number in the square at the bottom.

How many bees?

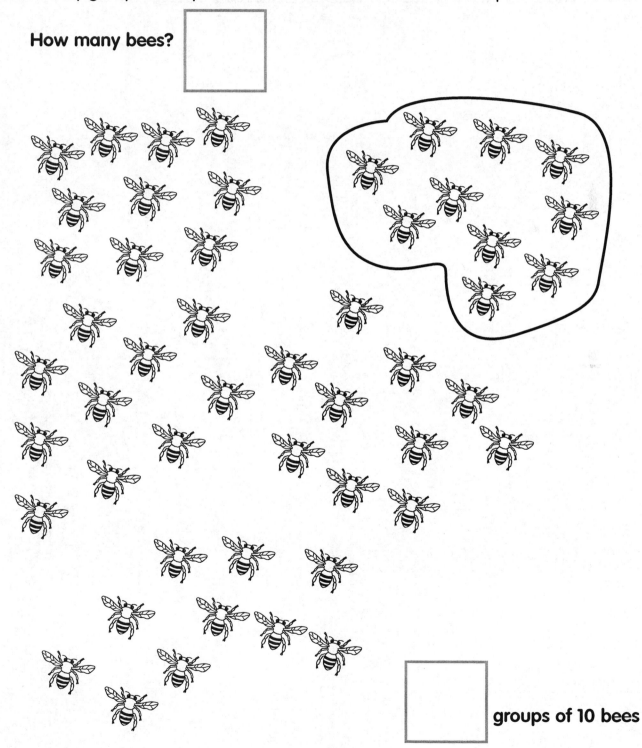

groups of 10 bees

Expanding Sentences

Directions: Write a word in each blank below to expand the sentences. Use the words from the Word Bank to help you.

Word Bank

big	fresh	spring
black	little	tall
clumsy	nice	young

1. The _____ cat is soft.

2. That _____ car is fast.

3. It's a lovely _____ day.

4. Did you see the _____ giraffe?

5. I can smell the _____ pizza.

6. The _____ boy fell down.

7. I saw the _____ elephant.

8. Trisha is a _____ , _____ girl.

Add or Subtract?

Directions: Read each math problem below. If you would add to solve the problem, circle **add**. If you would subtract, circle **subtract**.

1. I had 4 green apples. Jamie gave me 1 red apple. How many apples do I have in all?

    add   **subtract**

2. Gary found 1 yellow apple on the ground. He found 1 green apple on the fence. How many apples did Gary find in all?

    add   **subtract**

3. Miranda bought 3 small apples and 1 large apple. How many apples did Miranda buy in all?

    add   **subtract**

4. Charlie picked 4 apples. He gave 2 of them away. How many apples does Charlie have now?

    add   **subtract**

Beginning Sounds

Directions: Change the beginning sound of the underlined word to make a new word that completes the sentence. Use the correct word from the Word Bank.

Word Bank

dig	get	man	sun
dog	hat	sad	ten

1. The <u>cat</u> wore a _____.

2. The _____ went for a <u>jog</u>.

3. We had <u>fun</u> in the _____.

4. What did you _____ in the <u>net</u>?

5. A _____ had a <u>fan</u>.

6. The <u>pig</u> began to _____.

7. The <u>dad</u> was very _____.

8. There were _____ <u>men</u>.

Using a Ruler

Directions: Measure the objects below, using a ruler. Write the measurement of each object in inches.

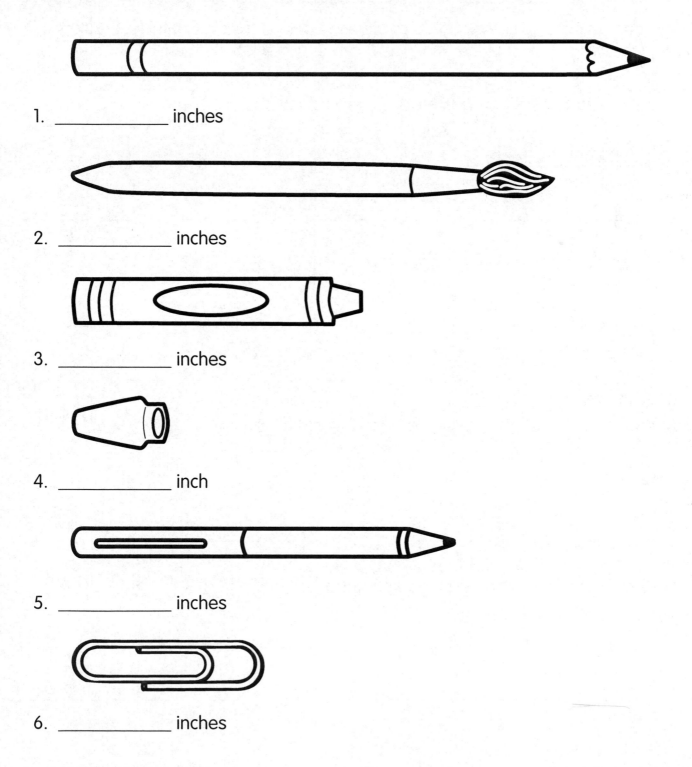

1. _____ inches

2. _____ inches

3. _____ inches

4. _____ inch

5. _____ inches

6. _____ inches

Just Tell Me

> **Statements** are telling sentences. They tell the reader something.

Directions: Write a statement for each situation below. Use a capital letter at the beginning and a period at the end. The first one has been started for you.

1. Write a statement that tells which toy is your favorite.

    My favorite toy is _____

    _____

2. Write a statement that tells what your favorite toy looks like.

    _____

    _____

3. Write a statement that tells what your favorite toy does.

    _____

    _____

4. Write a statement that tells how you got your favorite toy.

    _____

    _____

Name Poem

Directions: Write your name vertically in the boxes below. Then, write a word or phrase that begins with each letter in your name.

Example:

A	Always nice
B	Better at soccer than basketball
E	Extra smart

Barnyard Animals

Directions: Color the cow on the left side of the barn **black**. Color the cow on the right side of the barn **brown**. Color the chicken on the right **yellow** and the chicken on the left **red**. Leave the middle chicken **white**.

Groups of Five

Math

Directions: Count how many koalas there are below. Write this number at the top. Then, draw a line around each group of 5 koalas. The first one has been done for you. How many groups have you made? Write this number in the square at the bottom.

How many koalas?

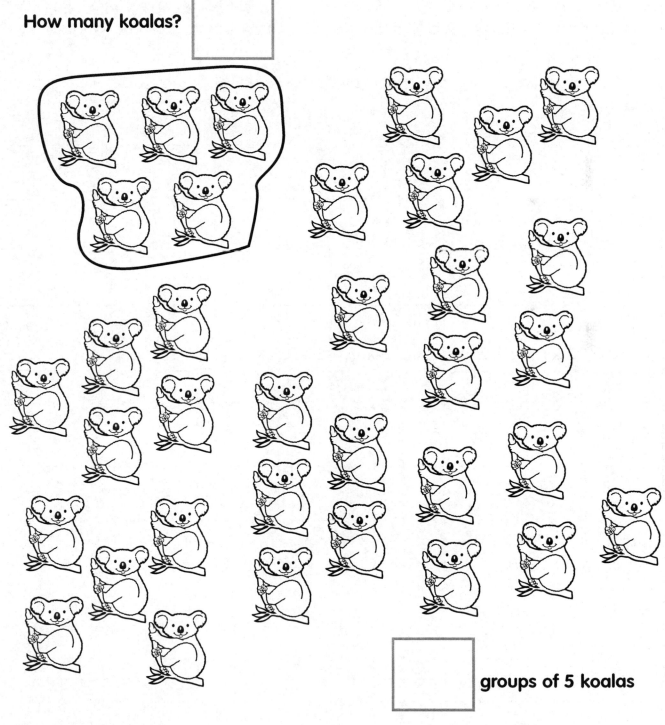

groups of 5 koalas

Just Ask Me

A **question** is a sentence that asks for information and needs an answer from the reader or listener.

Directions: Write a question for each situation below. Use a capital letter at the beginning and a question mark at the end. The first one has been done for you.

1. Write a question that asks what your family is having for lunch.

   What are we having for lunch?

   _____

2. Write a question that asks when you may eat lunch.

   _____

   _____

3. Write a question that asks if you may trade one food item.

   _____

   _____

4. Write a question that asks what you may drink with lunch.

   _____

   _____

Solve It

Directions: Solve the problems below. Show your work.

1. Stacy had 12 pieces of candy. She gave 6 pieces to Raul. How many pieces of candy does Stacy have left?

   Stacy has _____ pieces left.

2. Bea has 6 candles. She buys 5 more. How many candles does Bea now have?

   Bea now has _____ candles.

3. Manuel made 10 cakes. He sold 6 at the fair. How many cakes does Manuel have left?

   Manuel has _____ cakes left.

4. Omar can play 9 songs on his guitar. He has already played 4 songs. How many more songs can Omar play?

   Omar can play _____ more songs.

Ship Trip

Directions: Look at the scene. Color the seven objects that begin with the /sh/ sound.

Pick a Sign

Math

Directions: Draw > (greater than), < (less than), or = (equal to) in each box.

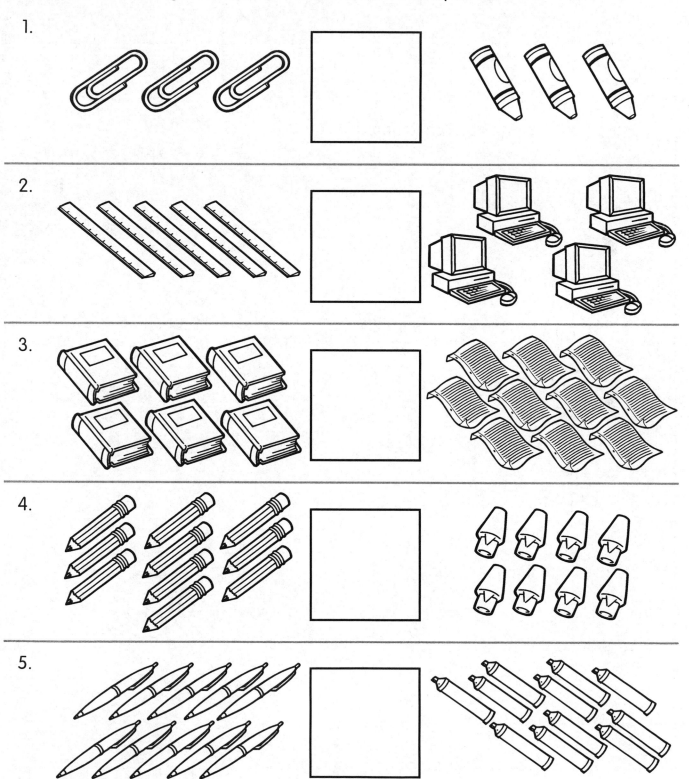

1.

2.

3.

4.

5.

End It

Directions: Write a period (.) or a question mark (?) at the end of each sentence.

1. The butterfly is beautiful _____

2. Have you seen an anteater before _____

3. You're my best friend _____

4. That's a nice shirt _____

5. How old are you _____

6. This is my dog _____

7. What time is it _____

8. Be careful not to fall down _____

9. Let's go to the library _____

10. Can you help me lift the box _____

Cloud Sums

Math

Directions: Circle the sets of numbers that add up to the sum in each cloud. There is more than one way to equal the sum.

1. **8**	2 + 2	5 + 4	3 + 5	7 + 1	6 + 2	4 + 3
2. **4**	2 + 2	3 + 2	4 + 0	5 + 1	3 + 1	0 + 4
3. **6**	6 + 0	2 + 5	4 + 2	3 + 3	5 + 1	6 + 2
4. **2**	2 + 0	3 + 1	4 + 1	1 + 1	0 + 2	1 + 2
5. **9**	4 + 6	3 + 6	1 + 8	1 + 9	8 + 2	9 + 0
6. **3**	3 + 1	2 + 0	3 + 0	2 + 1	0 + 3	1 + 2
7. **7**	6 + 1	2 + 5	3 + 5	6 + 3	4 + 3	7 + 0
8. **5**	2 + 2	5 + 0	3 + 2	1 + 4	4 + 2	2 + 3

Real or Make-Believe?

Directions: Read each sentence. Decide if it could be real or if it is make-believe. Fill in the correct bubble.

1. She had brown hair.

   ○ **real**

   ○ **make-believe**

2. He ate one thousand bananas for breakfast.

   ○ **real**

   ○ **make-believe**

3. Dad was mowing the lawn.

   ○ **real**

   ○ **make-believe**

4. The purple dog ran quickly.

   ○ **real**

   ○ **make-believe**

5. The cat barked at the dog.

   ○ **real**

   ○ **make-believe**

6. Mary baked a chocolate cake.

   ○ **real**

   ○ **make-believe**

7. We had a great time at the party.

   ○ **real**

   ○ **make-believe**

8. My brother is 200 years old.

   ○ **real**

   ○ **make-believe**

More or Less?

Directions: Look at the object in each box. Decide if the object would weigh **more than** one pound or **less than** one pound. Circle your answer.

---

1. **a paper clip**

   ☼ more than one pound

   ☼ less than one pound

2. **a cat**

   ☼ more than one pound

   ☼ less than one pound

3. **a chair**

   ☼ more than one pound

   ☼ less than one pound

4. **a door**

   ☼ more than one pound

   ☼ less than one pound

5. **an eraser**

   ☼ more than one pound

   ☼ less than one pound

6. **a person**

   ☼ more than one pound

   ☼ less than one pound

7. **a piece of paper**

   ☼ more than one pound

   ☼ less than one pound

8. **a computer**

   ☼ more than one pound

   ☼ less than one pound

9. **a pencil**

   ☼ more than one pound

   ☼ less than one pound

The Right Tool

Directions: Read each job description below, and write the correct measuring tool for the job on the line.

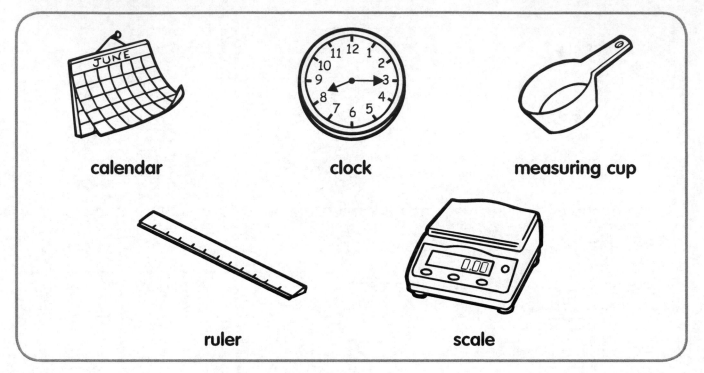

calendar

clock

measuring cup

ruler

scale

1. Logan is going on vacation on July 7, and he wants to know how long he has to wait. What measuring tool does he need? _____

2. Lyla wants to know how much her backpack weighs. What measuring tool does she need? _____

3. Miguel needs 8 inches of string for his art project. What measuring tool does he need? _____

4. Maya has a doctor's appointment at 2:00 p.m. today, and she wants to be on time. What measuring tool does she need? _____

5. Blake needs $\frac{1}{2}$ cup of sugar to make cookies. What measuring tool does he need? _____

Counting Up

Directions: Fill in the missing numbers on each side of the windmill, counting up by 2, 5, or 10.

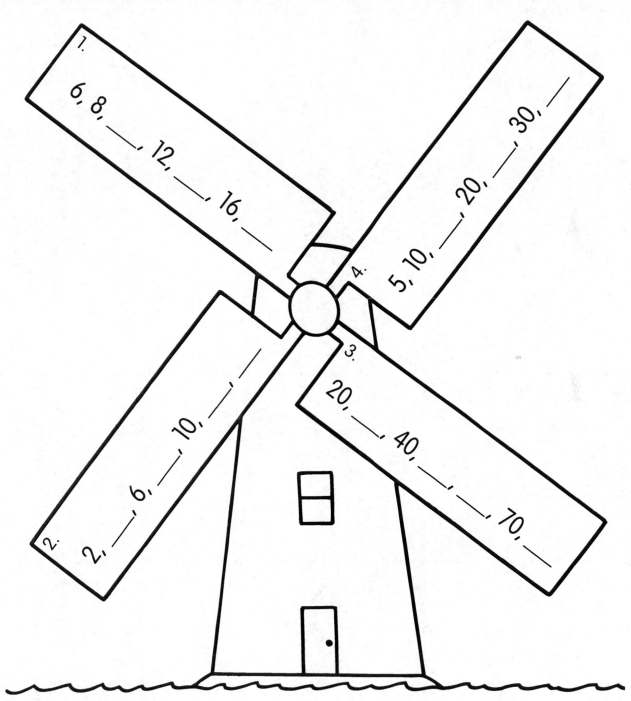

1. 6, 8, ___, 12, ___, 16, ___

2. 2, ___, 6, ___, 10, ___, ___

3. 20, ___, 40, ___, ___, 70, ___

4. 5, 10, ___, 20, ___, 30, ___

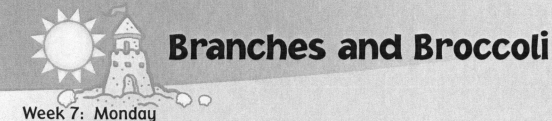

Branches and Broccoli

Directions: Color every object that begins with "br."

Rainy Day

Directions: Look at the picture below. Count each of the items listed, and put the number next to the word. Use these numbers to solve the math problems that follow.

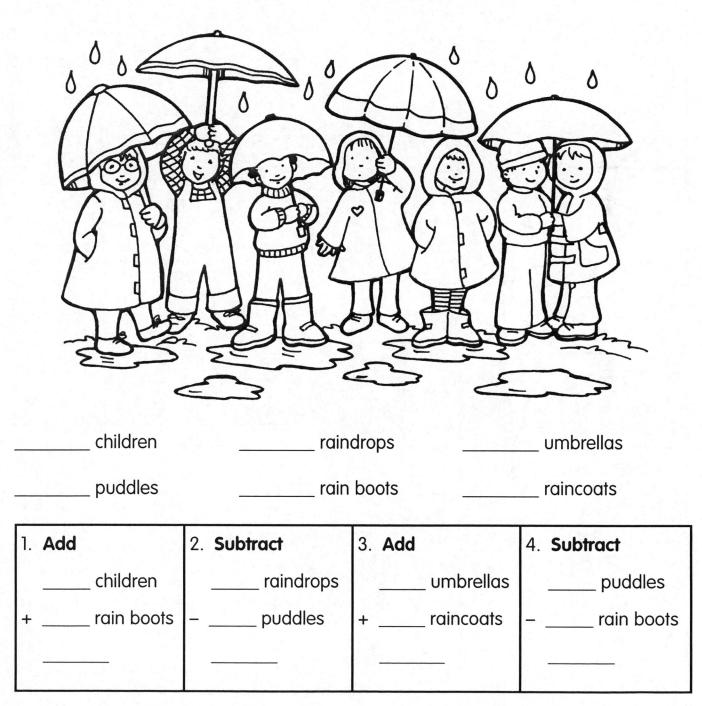

_____ children   _____ raindrops   _____ umbrellas

_____ puddles   _____ rain boots   _____ raincoats

1. **Add**	2. **Subtract**	3. **Add**	4. **Subtract**
_____ children	_____ raindrops	_____ umbrellas	_____ puddles
+ _____ rain boots	– _____ puddles	+ _____ raincoats	– _____ rain boots
_____	_____	_____	_____

Scrambled Eggs

Directions: The words in each egg can be put together to make a sentence. Write each sentence on the lines next to the egg. Be sure to use correct punctuation and capital letters.

all eggs lay birds

1. _____

   _____

watch you do birds

2. _____

   _____

some can birds talk

3. _____

   _____

bird feeder let's make a

4. _____

   _____

Counting Backward

Directions: Count backward, and write in the missing numbers.

1. 12, 11, _____ , 9, _____ , 7, _____

2. 12, _____ , 10, 9, _____

3. 12, _____ , 10, _____ , 8, _____

4. 8, 7, 6, _____ , _____ , 3, 2

5. 9, _____ , _____ , 6, 5

6. 7, _____ , 5, _____ , 3

7. 8, _____ , _____ , 5, _____

8. 11, 10, _____ , _____ , 7, _____

Rhyming Sentences

Directions: Complete each sentence with a word that rhymes with the underlined word. Use the words from the Word Bank to help you.

Word Bank

bee   book   box   fish   frog   hat

1. <u>Look</u> at the _____.

2. The <u>fox</u> is in a _____.

3. On the <u>log</u> sits a _____.

4. The <u>cat</u> wears a _____.

5. I <u>wish</u> I had a _____.

6. I <u>see</u> a _____.

Who's Driving?

Directions: Add each group of numbers on the cars below. Only one clown is driving a car whose sum equals 20. Which car is that clown driving? Color that car.

$2 + 3 + 7 + 5 =$

Car 1

$3 + 4 + 2 + 9 =$

Car 2

$9 + 3 + 2 + 6 =$

Car 3

$7 + 3 + 3 + 4 =$

Car 4

$2 + 7 + 9 + 7 =$

Car 5

$1 + 3 + 4 + 5 =$

Car 6

What's Outside?

Directions: Write about something you like to do outside. Then, draw a picture in the box below to go with your writing.

_____

_____

_____

_____

_____

What's Different?

Directions: Look at the two pictures below. Circle the five things that are different in the second picture.

Directions: Copy the picture one square at a time onto the bottom grid. Then, color your picture.

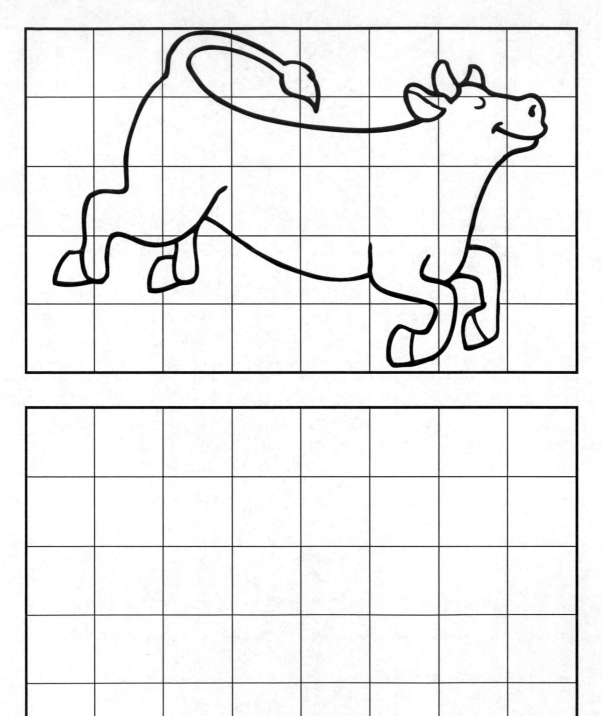

About How Long?

Directions: Read the list of activities below. Decide if each activity would take seconds, minutes, or hours to complete. Circle the correct response.

1. Go on a long hike.	seconds	minutes	hours
2. Write your name.	seconds	minutes	hours
3. Eat breakfast.	seconds	minutes	hours
4. Watch a movie.	seconds	minutes	hours
5. Do one jumping jack.	seconds	minutes	hours
6. Drive across your state.	seconds	minutes	hours
7. Write a letter to Grandma.	seconds	minutes	hours
8. Count to 10.	seconds	minutes	hours
9. Sing a song.	seconds	minutes	hours
10. Brush your teeth.	seconds	minutes	hours

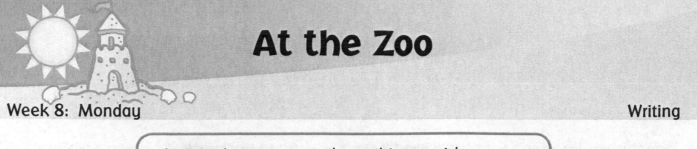

At the Zoo

A **noun** is a person, place, thing, or idea.
A **verb** says what a noun does or did.
An **adjective** tells about, or describes, a noun.

Directions: Think about the nouns, verbs, and adjectives you "see" at the zoo. Then, write them on the lines below.

Nouns: _____

_____

_____

Verbs: _____

_____

_____

Adjectives: _____

_____

_____

Which Symbol?

Directions: Write the **less than** or **greater than** symbol between the two numbers.

< the symbol for **less than**

> the symbol for **greater than**

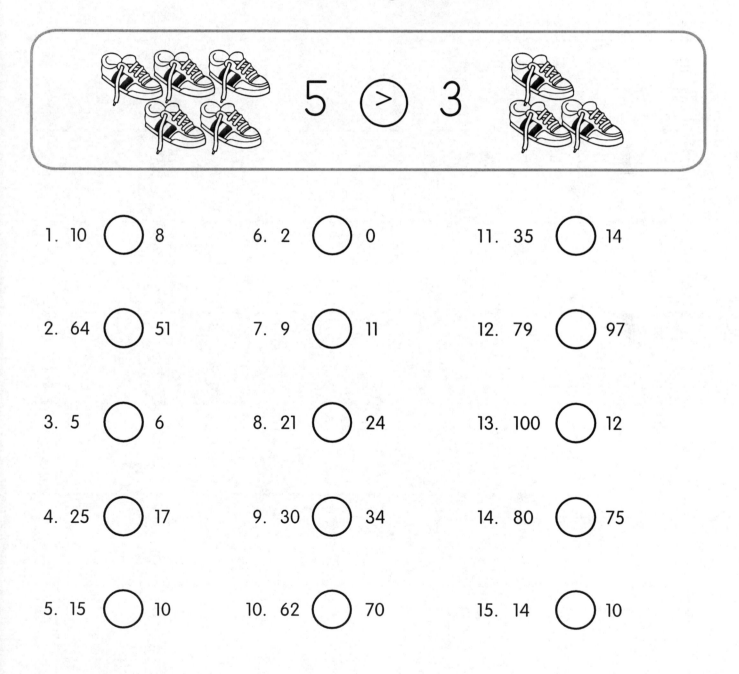

5 (>) 3

1. 10 ◯ 8

2. 64 ◯ 51

3. 5 ◯ 6

4. 25 ◯ 17

5. 15 ◯ 10

6. 2 ◯ 0

7. 9 ◯ 11

8. 21 ◯ 24

9. 30 ◯ 34

10. 62 ◯ 70

11. 35 ◯ 14

12. 79 ◯ 97

13. 100 ◯ 12

14. 80 ◯ 75

15. 14 ◯ 10

Fact or Opinion?

Directions: Read each statement. Decide if it is a fact or an opinion. Fill in the correct bubble.

1. There are seven days in a week.
   - ○ fact
   - ○ opinion

2. Her purple shirt is beautiful.
   - ○ fact
   - ○ opinion

3. A bicycle has two wheels.
   - ○ fact
   - ○ opinion

4. It is a long walk to school.
   - ○ fact
   - ○ opinion

5. A bird is the best kind of pet.
   - ○ fact
   - ○ opinion

6. *The Cat in the Hat* was written by Dr. Seuss.
   - ○ fact
   - ○ opinion

7. The radio is loud.
   - ○ fact
   - ○ opinion

8. Thanksgiving is in November.
   - ○ fact
   - ○ opinion

3-D Shapes

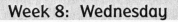

Directions: Say the name of the shape in the first box. Color the objects in the row that are the same shape as the shape in the first box.

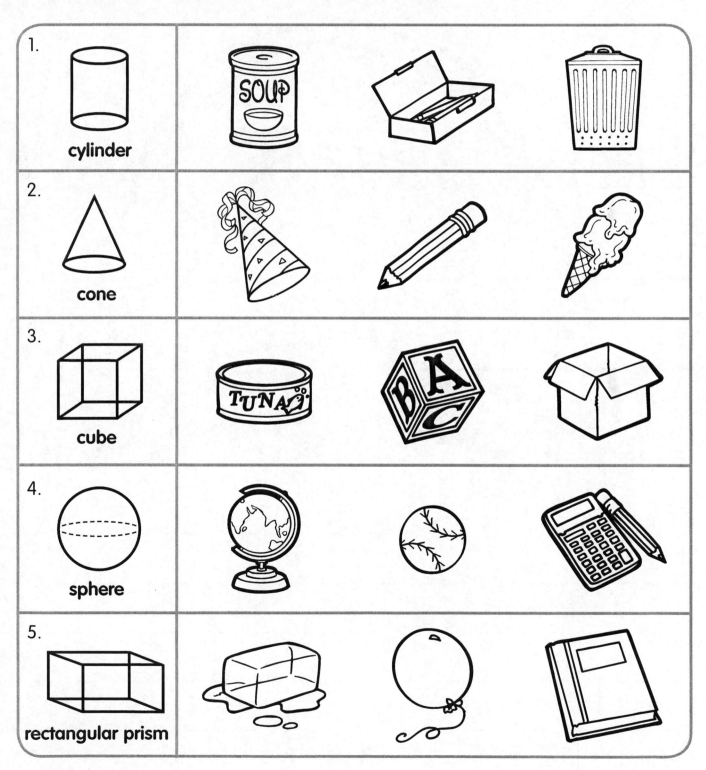

1. cylinder

2. cone

3. cube

4. sphere

5. rectangular prism

Who Lives Here?

Directions: What kinds of things live in caves? Draw a picture of a creature in the cave below. Write a story about your cave creature.

_____

_____

_____

_____

_____

Counting the Months

Directions: Use the Months of the Year chart to help you answer the questions below.

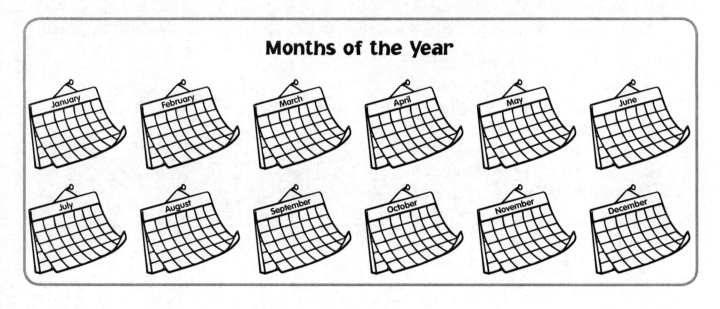

Months of the Year

January   February   March   April   May   June

July   August   September   October   November   December

1. How many months are in a year? _____

2. What is the first month of the year? _____

3. What is the last month of the year? _____

4. If it is May, how many months is it until November? _____

5. If it is August and Brian's birthday is two months away, what month is Brian's birthday in? _____

Read a Story

Directions: Read the story. Then, read the sentences underneath it. Write in the missing words from the story.

Jeff and Jill dug in the mud. Jeff dug and dug. His cap fell in the mud. Jill dug and dug. Her red hat fell in the mud. The cap was a mess. The red hat was a mess. "Yuck!" said Jeff and Jill. "Let's run and find Mom. She will fix the mess!"

1. Jeff and Jill dug in the _____.

2. His cap _____ in the mud.

3. The red _____ was a mess.

4. "_____!" said Jeff and Jill.

5. "Let's run and find _____."

6. "She will _____ the mess."

Challenge: Ask your child questions to help his or her comprehension of the story. Who was digging in the mud? What happened to the red hat?

Fishing for Toast

Directions: Use the code below to help you solve the riddle. Write each letter below the symbol to solve it.

What kind of fish goes well with toast?

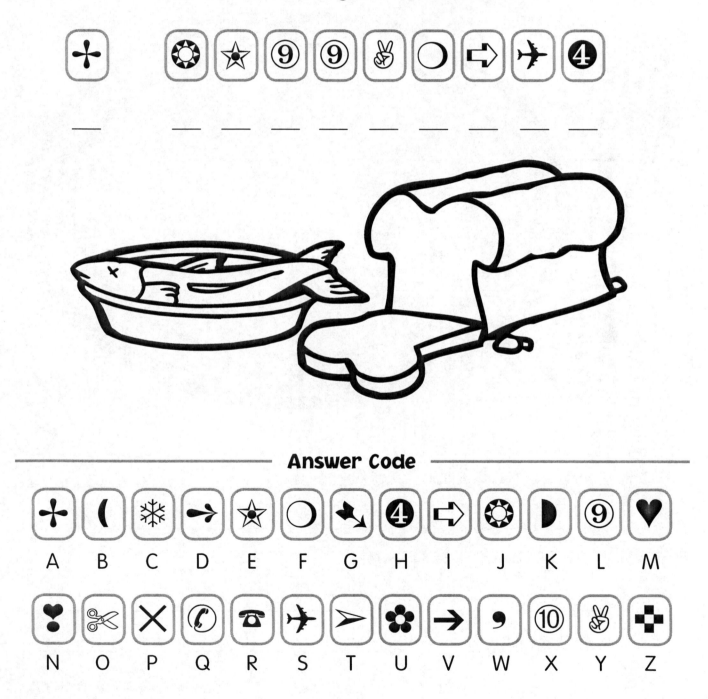

A JELLYFISH

Answer Code

✚	(	❄	➝	★	○	↙	➍	⇨	☀	◗	⑨	♥
A	B	C	D	E	F	G	H	I	J	K	L	M

♣	✂	✕	✆	☎	✈	➤	❀	→	,	⑩	✌	✚
N	O	P	Q	R	S	T	U	V	W	X	Y	Z

What's for Dinner?

Directions: Draw the food you ate for dinner last night on the plate. Then, answer the questions below.

1. This was/was not a nutritious meal because _____

_____.

2. It would be more nutritious if I added _____

_____

and did not eat _____

_____ which are not healthy.

All About Me

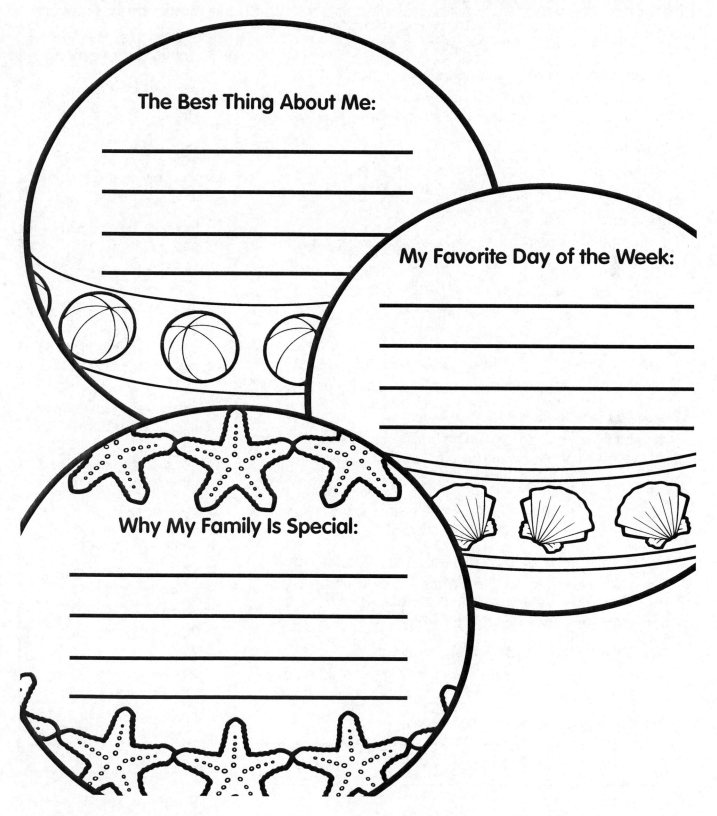

The Best Thing About Me:

_____

_____

_____

_____

My Favorite Day of the Week:

_____

_____

_____

_____

Why My Family Is Special:

_____

_____

_____

Summer Reading List

☼ **My Visit to the Aquarium** by Aliki

Aliki's detailed and colorful illustrations take the reader on a trip to the aquarium without leaving home.

☼ **Cloudy With a Chance of Meatballs** by Judi Barrett

Everything is great in the town of Chewandswallow, where it rains food three times a day, until the portions get bigger.

☼ **I Like Me!** by Nancy Carlson

This adorable story about a pig encourages children to like themselves and take good care of themselves.

☼ **Olivia** by Ian Falconer

Meet Olivia, a precocious, high-energy pig, in her first book of many.

☼ **Danny and the Dinosaur** by Syd Hoff

In this adventure tale, a dinosaur at the museum comes to life and spends the day with a young boy.

☼ **Harold and the Purple Crayon** by Crockett Johnson

Join Harold as he draws his way along an imaginative journey.

☼ **Leo the Late Bloomer** by Robert Kraus

Leo, the tiger, can't do everything his friends can, but his mom isn't worried. She knows he'll catch up in his own time.

☼ **Barn Dance!** by Bill Martin Jr.

While the farmer sleeps, the animals gather in the barn to kick up their hooves as the scarecrow plays his fiddle.

☼ **Listen to the Wind** by Greg Mortenson and Susan L. Roth

This children's version of *Three Cups of Tea*, tells the story of Greg Mortenson's experience in Pakistan and his determination to build a school there.

☼ **Tikki Tikki Tembo** retold by Arlene Mosel

A Chinese folktale, this story is about a boy who falls in a well and how his long name delays his rescue.

☼ **The Paper Bag Princess** by Robert N. Munsch

In this fairy-tale story, a brave princess sets off to rescue her prince when he is prince-napped by a dragon just before their wedding.

Making the Most of Summertime Reading

When reading these books with your child, you may wish to ask the questions below. The sharing of questions and answers will enhance and improve your child's reading comprehension skills.

☼ Why did you pick this book to read?

☼ Name a character from the story that you like. Why do you like him or her?

☼ Where does the story take place? Do you want to go there?

☼ Name a problem from the story. How is it solved?

☼ What is the best part of the story so far? Describe it!

☼ What do you think is going to happen next in the story? Guess!

☼ Who are the important characters in the story? Why are they important?

☼ What is the book about?

☼ What are two things you have learned by reading this book?

☼ Would you tell your friend to read this book? Why or why not?

Summer Reading List
(cont.)

- **Dewey: There's a Cat in the Library!** by Vicki Myron and Bret Witter
  After being abandoned in the return-book slot, a young kitten becomes the official library cat. Based on a true story.

- **Fancy Nancy: Explorer Extraordinaire!** by Jane O'Connor
  Fancy Nancy is as fancy as ever as she explores the great outdoors, including butterflies, spiders, ladybugs, wildflowers, birds, and more.

- **Curious George Goes to the Beach** by H. A. Rey
  Join everyone's favorite monkey and the man with the yellow hat for a day at the beach. Everything is going fine until a seagull flies away with something valuable. What will George do?

- **Henry and Mudge: The First Book** by Cynthia Rylant
  Henry is lonely, so he asks his parents for a dog. His new puppy quickly becomes a very large dog and his best friend.

- **Skippyjon Jones** by Judy Schachner
  This funny story introduces Skippyjon Jones, a Siamese kitten with a vivid imagination.

- **The True Story of the Three Little Pigs** by Jon Scieszka
  Finally, after years of being ignored, the wolf gets his chance to give his side of this classic tale.

- **Where the Wild Things Are** by Maurice Sendak
  After being sent to his room without dinner, a boy finds himself on an interesting adventure among the wild things.

- **Sheep in a Jeep** by Nancy E. Shaw
  In this rhyming adventure, five foolish sheep in a jeep head off on a road trip.

- **Sylvester and the Magic Pebble** by William Steig
  Sylvester finds a magic pebble that makes all his wishes come true, but when he encounters a lion, he makes an unfortunate wish that separates him from his family. What will he do?

- **The Polar Express** by Chris Van Allsburg
  Take a magical journey to the North Pole aboard the *Polar Express*.

- **Alexander and the Terrible, Horrible, No Good, Very Bad Day** by Judith Viorst
  Everyone has bad days, but Alexander's is so bad that he wants to "move to Australia."

- **Ira Sleeps Over** by Bernard Waber
  Ira is excited to spend the night at his friend's house until he gets nervous about sleeping without his teddy bear.

- **Falling for Rapunzel** by Leah Wilcox
  You'll laugh aloud at the silly twists in this unusual retelling of the classic fairy tale.

- **Pigs Make Me Sneeze** by Mo Willems
  Find out what happens when Gerald the elephant thinks he is allergic to his best friend Piggie.

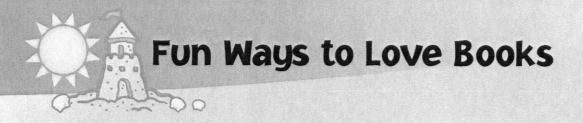

Fun Ways to Love Books

Here are some fun ways that your child can expand on his or her reading. Most of these ideas will involve both you and your child; however, the wording has been directed towards your child because we want him or her to be inspired to love books.

Design a Bookmark

You can design a bookmark for your favorite book, and then use it in other books to remind you of a great reading experience. Use a strip of colorful paper and include the title, the author, and a picture of something that happened in the book.

Book Chain

Create a book chain to link your favorite books together. First, cut out strips of colored paper. On one strip, write down the name of your favorite book. On the other, describe your favorite part of the story. Staple or tape the strips of paper together to form a circle. Do this for each book you read, and link all of your books together. Use the chain to decorate your room.

Always Take a Book

Maybe you've had to wait with your parents in line at the post office or in the vet's waiting room with nothing to do. If you get into the habit of bringing a book with you wherever you go, you'll always have something exciting to do! Train yourself to always take a good book. You might want to carry a small backpack or shoulder bag—something that allows you to carry a book easily from place to place. Don't forget a bookmark!

Novel Foods

What foods do the characters in your book eat? What do they drink? What are their favorite foods? Get a better sense of your characters' tastes by cooking their favorite foods. Some characters love sweet things, like cookies and ice cream. Other characters like hamburgers and pizza. Decide what foods your characters love. With your parents' help, locate appropriate recipes on the Internet or in books. Then, make up a grocery list. Buy groceries and gather necessary materials, such as mixing bowls, spoons, and pans. Cook your characters' favorite foods by yourself or with friends.

Story Time for Pets

Some cats and dogs enjoy being read to. They appreciate the verbal attention—especially if it's accompanied by a loving scratch behind the ears. Choose your favorite book, and read it to your pet. Notice whether he or she particularly likes being read to. Your dog may tilt its head and raise its ears, trying to understand what you are reading. A cat may rub its cheek against you or climb into your lap as you read. You might even want to read a special book about a dog or cat to your pet.

Bookmark Your Words

Make summertime reading lots of fun with these reading log glasses. Have your child fill in the glasses after his or her daily reading. For younger children, you may need to help them fill in the information. Or, as an alternative, they can draw a picture of something they read from that day. Once they have completed the glasses, they can cut them out and use them as bookmarks.

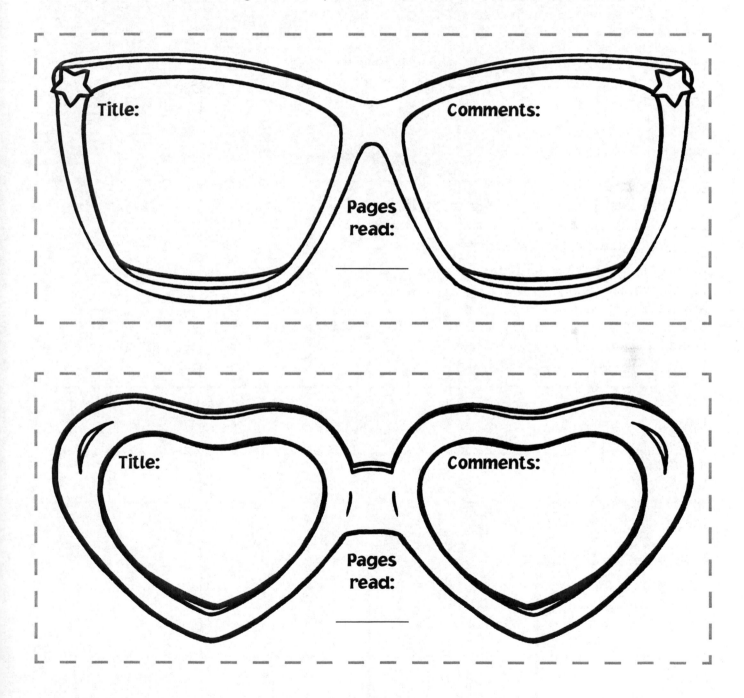

This page may be reproduced as many times as needed.

Read-Together Chart

Does your father read books to you before bed? Perhaps your mother reads to the family at breakfast? Your grandparents may enjoy reading books to you after school or on the weekends. You and your family members can create a Read-Together Chart and fill it in to keep track of all the books you've read together.

Here are two Read-Together Charts. The first one is a sample. The second one has been left blank, so you can add your own categories and books.

Sample Chart

Book We Read	Who Read It?	Summary	Our Review
The Secret Garden	My older sister read it to me.	It's about a spoiled girl who learns to love nature and people.	We like this book. The characters are funny, and the illustrations are beautiful!

Your Chart

This page may be reproduced as many times as needed.

Journal Topics

Choose one of these journal topics each day. Make sure you add enough detail so someone else reading this will clearly be able to know at least four of the following:

☼ who	☼ what	☼ when	☼ where	☼ why	☼ how

1. My favorite birthday was . . .
2. My best friend is . . .
3. If I were a scuba diver, I would see . . .
4. My last vacation was to . . .
5. A famous person I like is . . .
6. A question I would like to ask my principal is . . .
7. A movie star I like is . . .
8. I live in . . .
9. My kindergarten teacher deserves to be "Teacher of the Year" because . . .
10. When I take a walk outside, I hear . . .
11. My favorite food is . . .
12. Something that makes me happy is . . .
13. If I wrote a book, it would be about . . .
14. My favorite movie is . . .
15. A lion would be a bad pet because . . .
16. When I get a gift, I feel . . .
17. If I could be any animal, I would be . . .
18. If I went to the moon, I would see . . .
19. In the summer, I like to . . .
20. My favorite dessert is . . .
21. When I sleep, I dream about . . .
22. During the weekend, I like to . . .
23. When I am sad, I . . .
24. My favorite song is . . .
25. I usually forget to . . .

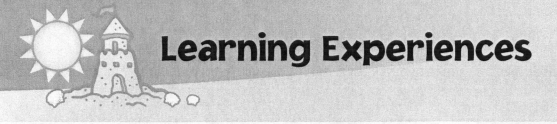

Learning Experiences

Here are some fun, low-cost activities that you can do with your child. You'll soon discover that these activities can be stimulating, educational, and complementary to the other exercises in this book.

Flash Cards

Make up all types of flash cards. Depending on your child's interests and grade level, these cards might feature enrichment words, math problems, or states and capitals. You can create them yourself with markers or on a computer. Let your child help cut pictures out of magazines and glue them on. Then, find a spot outdoors, and go through the flash cards with your child.

Project Pantry

Find a spot in your house where you can store supplies. This might be a closet or a bin that stays in one spot. Get some clean paint cans or buckets. Fill them with all types of craft and art supplies. Besides the typical paints, markers, paper, scissors, and glue, include some more unusual things, such as tiles, artificial flowers, and wrapping paper. This way, whenever you and your child want to do a craft project, you have everything you need at that moment.

The Local Library

Check out everything that your local library has to offer. Most libraries offer summer reading programs with various incentives. Spend an afternoon choosing and then reading books together.

Collect Something

Let your child choose something to collect that is free or inexpensive, such as paper clips or buttons. If your child wants to collect something that might be impractical, like horses, find pictures in magazines or catalogs, and have your child cut them out and start a picture collection.

Grocery Store Trip

Instead of making a trip to the grocery store a chore, make it a challenge. Even with nonreaders, you can have them help you find items on the shelf. Start by giving your child a list of his or her own. Review the list before you go. For nonreaders, you might want to cut pictures from ads. Many stores even have smaller shopping carts, so your child can have his or her own cart to fill. Once you get to an aisle where you know there is something on your child's list, prompt him or her to find the item. You may have to help your child get something down from a shelf.

Eating the Alphabet

Wouldn't it be fun to eat the alphabet? During the course of the summer, see how many fresh fruits and vegetables you can eat from A to Z. You and your child can make a poster or a chart with the letters A–Z on it. Once you have the chart, each time your child eats a fruit or vegetable, write it next to the matching letter of the alphabet. You can also let your child draw a picture of what he or she has eaten.

How Much Does It Cost?

If you go out for a meal, have your child help total the bill. Write down the cost of each person's meal. Then, have your child add them all together. You can vary this and make it much simpler by having your child just figure out the cost of an entrée and a drink or the cost of three desserts. You might want to round the figures first.

Nature Scavenger Hunt

Take a walk, go to a park, or hike in the mountains. But before you go, create a scavenger hunt list for your child. This can consist of all sorts of things found in nature. Make sure your child has a bag to carry everything he or she finds. (Be sure to check ahead of time about the rules or laws regarding removing anything.) You might include things like a leaf with pointed edges, a speckled rock, and a twig with two small limbs on it. Take a few minutes to look at all the things your child has collected, and check them off the list.

Measure It!

Using a ruler, tape measure, or yardstick is one way to see how tall something is. Start with your child, and find out how tall he or she is. Now, find other things to measure and compare. Find out how much shorter a book is compared to your child, or discover how much taller the door is than your child. To measure things that can't be measured with a ruler, take some string and stretch it around the object. Cut or mark it where it ends. Then, stretch the string next to the ruler or tape measure to find out how long it is. Your child may be surprised at how different something that is the same number of inches looks when the shape is different.

Take a Trip, and Keep a Journal

If you are going away during the summer, have your child keep a journal. Depending on his or her age, this can take a different look. A young child can collect postcards and paste them into a blank journal. He or she can also draw pictures of places he or she is visiting. An older child can keep a traditional journal and draw pictures. Your child can also do a photo-journal if a camera is available for him or her to use.

Be a Scientist

Without your child's knowledge, put a ball inside a box, and cover it with a lid. Call in your child, and tell him or her to act like a scientist. He or she will need to ask questions and try to figure out answers like a scientist would. If your child is having a hard time asking questions, you may need to help. Some questions to ask include, "What do you think is inside the box?" and "How do you know?" Have your child shake the box and see if he or she can figure it out.

Web Sites

Math Web Sites

☼ **AAA Math:** http://www.aaamath.com
This site contains hundreds of pages of basic math skills divided by grade or topic.

☼ **AllMath.com:** http://www.allmath.com
This site has math flashcards, biographies of mathematicians, and a math glossary.

☼ **Coolmath.com:** http://www.coolmath.com
Explore this amusement park of mathematics! Have fun with the interactive activities.

☼ **Mrs. Glosser's Math Goodies:** http://www.mathgoodies.com
This is a free educational Web site featuring interactive worksheets, puzzles, and more!

Reading and Writing Web Sites

☼ **Aesop's Fables:** http://www.umass.edu/aesop
This site has almost forty of the fables. Both traditional and modern versions are presented.

☼ **American Library Association:** http://ala.org
Visit this site to find out both the past and present John Newbery Medal and Randolph Caldecott Medal winners.

☼ **Book Adventure:** http://www.bookadventure.com
This site features a free reading incentive program dedicated to encouraging children in grades K–8 to read.

☼ **Fairy Godmother:** http://www.fairygodmother.com
This site will capture your child's imagination and spur it on to wonderful creativity.

☼ **Rhymezone:** http://www.rhymezone.com
Type in the word you want to rhyme. If there is a rhyming word to match your word, you'll find it here.

General Web Sites

☼ **Animal Photos:** http://nationalzoo.si.edu
This site offers wonderful pictures of animals, as well as virtual zoo visits.

☼ **Dinosaur Guide:** http://dsc.discovery.com/dinosaurs
This is an interactive site on dinosaurs that goes beyond just learning about the creatures.

☼ **The Electronic Zoo:** http://netvet.wustl.edu/e-zoo.htm
This site has links to thousands of animal sites covering every creature under the sun!

☼ **Maggie's Earth Adventures:** http://www.missmaggie.org
Join Maggie and her dog, Dude, on a wonderful Earth adventure.

☼ **Sesame Street:** http://www.sesamestreet.org
There is no shortage of fun for children at Sesame Street.

Printing Chart

numbers 1-100

1	2	3	4	5	6	7	8	9	10
11	12	13	14	15	16	17	18	19	20
21	22	23	24	25	26	27	28	29	30
31	32	33	34	35	36	37	38	39	40
41	42	43	44	45	46	47	48	49	50
51	52	53	54	55	56	57	58	59	60
61	62	63	64	65	66	67	68	69	70
71	72	73	74	75	76	77	78	79	80
81	82	83	84	85	86	87	88	89	90
91	92	93	94	95	96	97	98	99	100

Addition Chart

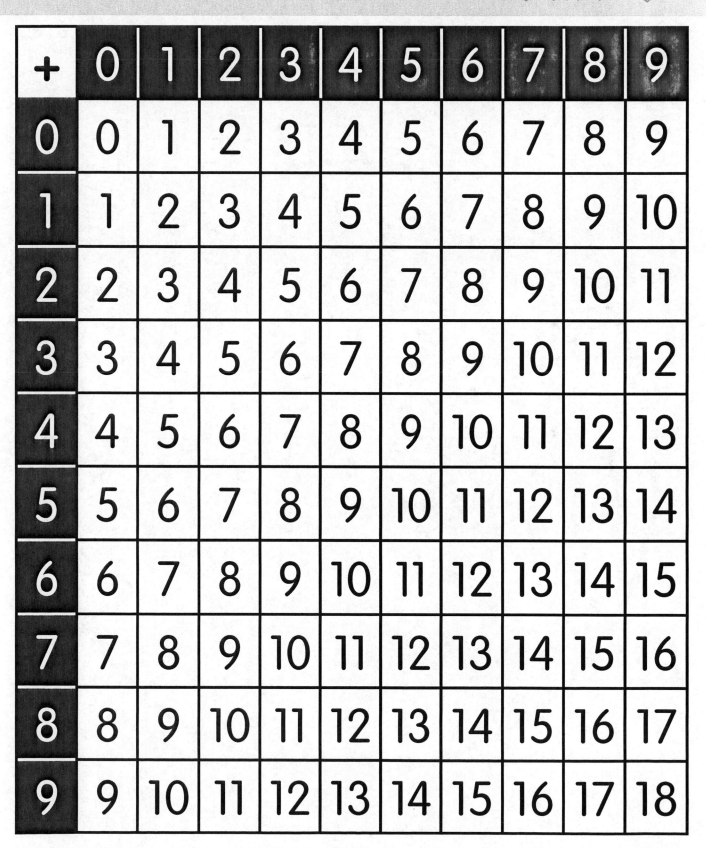

+	0	1	2	3	4	5	6	7	8	9
0	0	1	2	3	4	5	6	7	8	9
1	1	2	3	4	5	6	7	8	9	10
2	2	3	4	5	6	7	8	9	10	11
3	3	4	5	6	7	8	9	10	11	12
4	4	5	6	7	8	9	10	11	12	13
5	5	6	7	8	9	10	11	12	13	14
6	6	7	8	9	10	11	12	13	14	15
7	7	8	9	10	11	12	13	14	15	16
8	8	9	10	11	12	13	14	15	16	17
9	9	10	11	12	13	14	15	16	17	18

Clock Pattern

Use this clock pattern to practice telling time. Ask your parents to photocopy this page and cut out the hour and minute hands below. Then, have them attach the hands to the center dot on the clock's face using a brad (paper fastener). Or, as an alternative, you can use a small paper clip for the hour hand and a large paper clip for the minute hand.

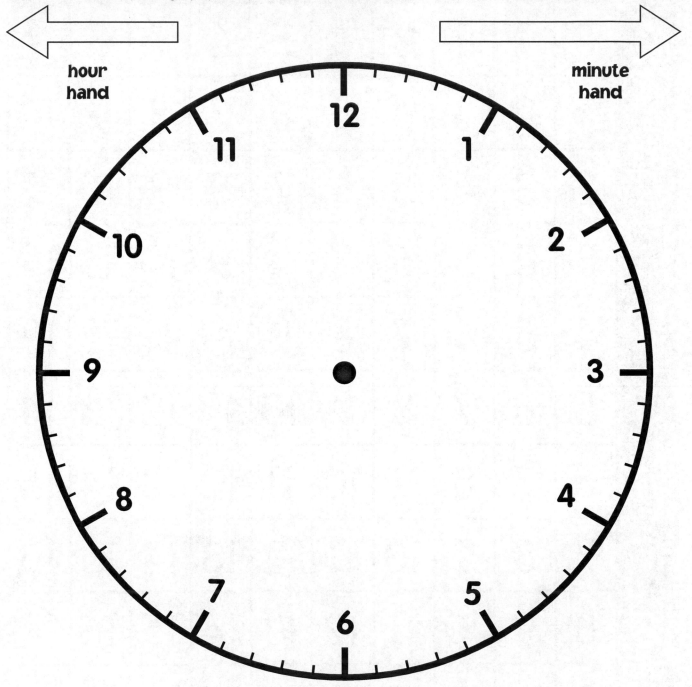

This page may be reproduced as many times as needed.

Money Chart

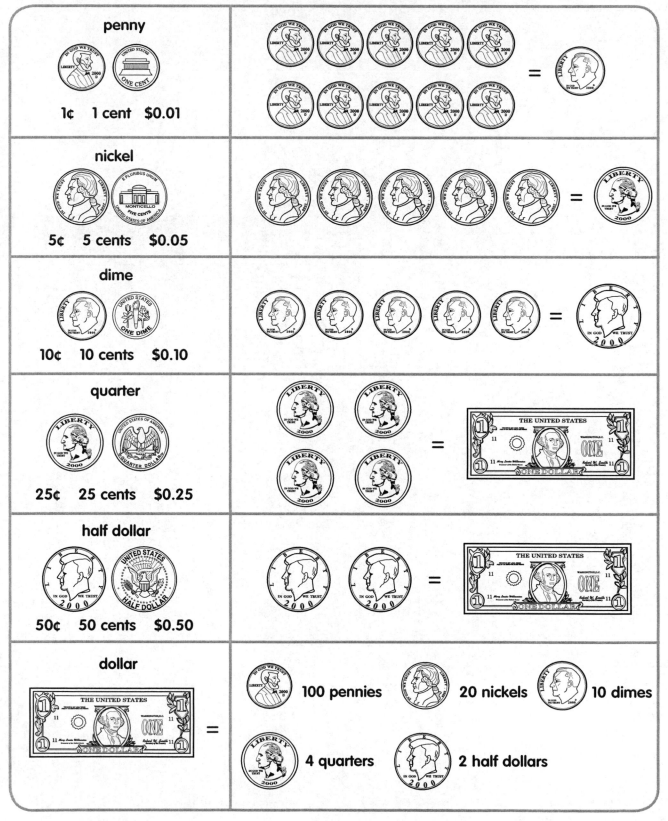

penny

1¢   1 cent $0.01

nickel

5¢   5 cents $0.05

dime

10¢   10 cents $0.10

quarter

25¢   25 cents $0.25

half dollar

50¢   50 cents $0.50

dollar

= 100 pennies   20 nickels   10 dimes

4 quarters   2 half dollars

Answer Key

Page 11
1. 6, six
2. 2, two
3. 7, seven
4. 4, four
5. 3, three
6. 1, one
7. 5, five
8. 8, eight

Page 12
1. fan, can, man
2. fin, pin, win
3. jet, net, vet
4. mop, pop, hop

Page 13
1. 11 pairs or 22
2. 14
3. 17
4. 13
5. 15
6. 18
7. 12
8. 16

Page 14
1. big
2. smelly
3. three
4. beautiful
5. quiet
6. hot
7. cute
8. round

Page 15

1. 3 + 2 = 5	4. 4 + 2 = 6
2. 6 + 1 = 7	5. 3 + 0 = 3
3. 5 + 3 = 8	6. 4 + 4 = 8

Page 16
1. cat
2. tap
3. bed
4. pen
5. wig
6. pin
7. log
8. mop
9. tub
10. run

Page 17

	1	2	3	4	5	6
pigs	■	■	■			
cows	■	■	■	■		
sheep	■	■	■	■	■	
chickens	■	■	■	■		
dogs	■	■				

1. sheep
2. 4
3. 20

Page 18
Answers will vary.

Page 19
Answers will vary. Possible answers:
1. books
2. fly
3. run
4. hot
5. away
6. glee

Page 20
1. plate
2. car
3. shoe
4. can of soup
5. cloud and lightning bolt

Answer Key (cont.)

Page 21
1. 15 − **10** = 5
2. 13 − **9** = 4
3. 14 − **6** = 8

Page 22
1. chased
2. twinkle
3. watched
4. set
5. swim
6. sings
7. eat
8. threw

Page 23
☼ 12 pizza toppings
☼ 16 ice cubes

Page 24
1. fan, fin
2. pin, pan
3. net, nut
4. leg, log
5. cot, cat
6. map, mop
7. dig or dug, dog
8. bug, bag

Page 25

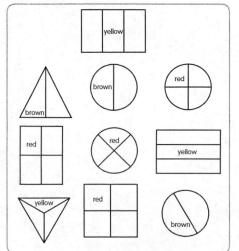

Page 26
The Lost Cat
This morning, my cat got lost. First, I looked under my bed. Then, I looked under the table. Finally, I looked in the closet. There was my cat sitting in the closet!

Page 27
1. 16
2. 14
3. 12
4. 17

Page 28
1. Little
2. Three
3. Baby
4. Old

Page 29
1. Color the apple, banana, and pear; put an **X** on the carrot.
2. Color the hammer, screwdriver, and wrench; put an **X** on the stapler.
3. Color the sheep, horse, and cow; put an **X** on the tiger.
4. Color the sun, lamp, and flashlight; put an **X** on the pencil.
5. Color the bus, car, and truck; put an **X** on the wagon.
6. Color the seagull, stork, and hummingbird; put an **X** on the lizard.

Page 30
1. feathers
2. hair (color)
3. scales
4. hair (color)
5. hair (color)
6. feathers
7. scales
8. hair (color)
9. scales

Answer Key *(cont.)*

Page 31
1. 5 o'clock
2. 10 o'clock
3. 9 o'clock
4. 2 o'clock
5. 3 o'clock
6. 12 o'clock

Page 32
1. yes
2. no
3. yes
4. no
5. no
6. no
7. yes
8. yes
9. no
10. no

Page 33
1. 5 – 2 = 3
2. 6 – 4 = 2
3. 4 – 1 = 3
4. 7 – 6 = 1
5. 5 – 5 = 0
6. 6 – 3 = 3

Page 34
1. My
2. Can
3. I
4. We
5. She
6. There
7. Are
8. Her

Page 35

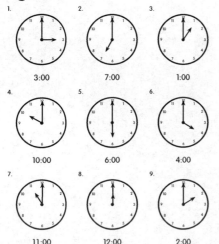

Page 36
1. bat
2. pot
3. saw
4. orange
5. bowl

Page 37
1. Sunday
2. Monday
3. three days
4. Tuesday and Thursday
5. Saturday

Page 38
Answers will vary.

Page 39
1. cold
2. light
3. on
4. under
5. low
6. out
7. near
8. straight
9. down
10. sad
11. dirty
12. short

Page 41
1. 7
2. 9
3. 4
4. 6

Page 42
1. The snake slithers.
2. The rabbit jumps.
3. The lion roars.
4. The dog barks.
5. The bee buzzes.
6. The bird chirps.
7. The cow moos.

Answer Key *(cont.)*

Page 43

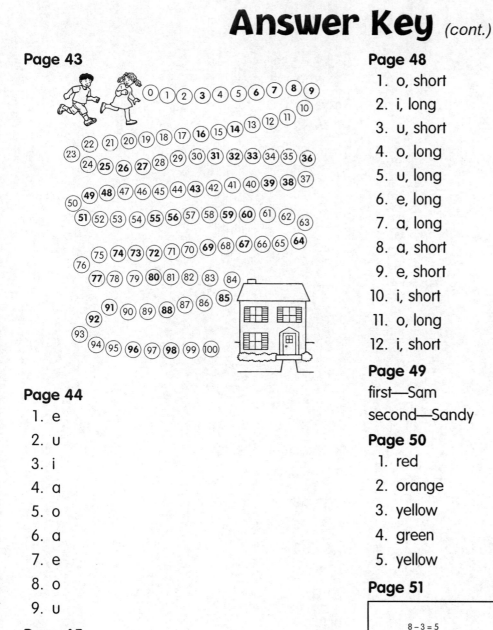

Page 44

1. e
2. u
3. i
4. a
5. o
6. a
7. e
8. o
9. u

Page 45

1. 6   3. 6
2. 1   4. 7

Page 46

Answers will vary.

Page 47

1. triangle
2. hexagon
3. circle
4. pentagon
5. rectangle
6. square

Page 48

1. o, short
2. i, long
3. u, short
4. o, long
5. u, long
6. e, long
7. a, long
8. a, short
9. e, short
10. i, short
11. o, long
12. i, short

Page 49

first—Sam   third—Sally
second—Sandy   last—Sarah

Page 50

1. red   6. blue
2. orange   7. red
3. yellow   8. yellow
4. green   9. green
5. yellow   10. blue

Page 51

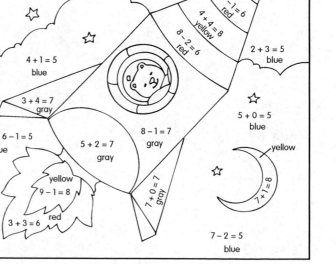

Answer Key (cont.)

Page 52
1. The spider sees a fly.
2. The rats paint a picture.
3. The kid spits seeds.
4. The pets stomp on ants.

Page 53
- 50 bees
- Groups of 10 will vary.
- 5 groups of 10 bees

Page 54
Answers will vary. Possible answers:
1. black
2. little
3. spring
4. tall
5. fresh
6. clumsy
7. big
8. nice, young

Page 55
1. add
2. add
3. add
4. subtract

Page 56
1. hat
2. dog
3. sun
4. get
5. man
6. dig
7. sad
8. ten

Page 57
1. 6 inches
2. 5 inches
3. 3 inches
4. 1 inch
5. 4 inches
6. 2 inches

Page 58
Answers will vary.

Page 59
Answers will vary.

Page 60

Page 61
- 35 koalas
- Groups of 5 will vary.
- 7 groups of 5 koalas

Page 62
Answers will vary.

Page 63
1. 6
2. 11
3. 4
4. 5

Page 64
The following objects should be colored: shirt, ship, shark, shrimp, shells, shadow, and sheep.

Page 65
1. =
2. >
3. <
4. >
5. <

Page 66
1. .
2. ?
3. .
4. .
5. ?
6. .
7. ?
8. .
9. .
10. ?

Answer Key (cont.)

Page 67
1. 3 + 5, 7 + 1, 6 + 2
2. 2 + 2, 4 + 0, 3 + 1, 0 + 4
3. 6 + 0, 4 + 2, 3 + 3, 5 + 1
4. 2 + 0, 1 + 1, 0 + 2
5. 3 + 6, 1 + 8, 9 + 0
6. 3 + 0, 2 + 1, 0 + 3, 1 + 2
7. 6 + 1, 2 + 5, 4 + 3, 7 + 0
8. 5 + 0, 3 + 2, 1 + 4, 2 + 3

Page 68
1. real
2. make-believe
3. real
4. make-believe
5. make-believe
6. real
7. real
8. make-believe

Page 69
1. less than one pound
2. more than one pound
3. more than one pound
4. more than one pound
5. less than one pound
6. more than one pound
7. less than one pound
8. more than one pound
9. less than one pound

Page 70
1. calendar
2. scale
3. ruler
4. clock
5. measuring cup

Page 71
1. 6, 8, **10**, 12, **14**, 16, **18**
2. 2, **4**, 6, **8**, 10, **12**, 14
3. 20, **30**, 40, **50**, **60**, 70, **80**
4. 5, 10, **15**, 20, **25**, 30, **35**

Page 72
The following objects should be colored: bread, branch, brush, broom, broccoli, and bride.

Page 73
7 children

6 puddles

10 raindrops

4 rain boots

5 umbrellas

4 raincoats

1. 7 + 4 = 11
2. 10 − 6 = 4
3. 5 + 4 = 9
4. 6 − 4 = 2

Page 74
1. All birds lay eggs.
2. Do you watch birds? *or* You do watch birds.
3. Some birds can talk. *or* Can some birds talk?
4. Let's make a bird feeder.

Page 75
1. 12, 11, **10**, 9, **8**, 7, **6**
2. 12, **11**, 10, 9, **8**
3. 12, **11**, 10, **9**, 8, **7**
4. 8, 7, 6, **5**, **4**, 3, 2
5. 9, **8**, **7**, 6, 5
6. 7, **6**, 5, **4**, 3
7. 8, **7**, 6, 5, **4**
8. 11, 10, **9**, **8**, 7, **6**

Page 76
1. book
2. box
3. frog
4. hat
5. fish
6. bee

Answer Key *(cont.)*

Page 77
Car 1 = 17
Car 2 = 18
Car 3 = 20 (should be colored)
Car 4 = 17
Car 5 = 25
Car 6 = 13

Page 78
Answers will vary.

Page 79
In the second picture, there is a cloud in the sky, there is one extra tuft of grass, and there is one extra bubble. Also, the boy is wearing a bracelet and a T-shirt with a lightning bolt on it.

Page 81
1. hours
2. seconds
3. minutes
4. hours
5. seconds
6. hours
7. minutes
8. seconds
9. minutes
10. minutes

Page 82
Answers will vary.

Page 83
1. >
2. >
3. <
4. >
5. >
6. >
7. <
8. <
9. <
10. <
11. >
12. <
13. >
14. >
15. >

Page 84
1. fact
2. opinion
3. fact
4. opinion
5. opinion
6. fact
7. opinion
8. fact

Page 85
1. can of soup, trash can
2. party hat, ice-cream cone
3. block, box
4. globe, baseball
5. ice, book

Page 86
Answers will vary.

Page 87
1. twelve months
2. January
3. December
4. six months
5. October

Page 88
1. mud
2. fell
3. hat
4. Yuck
5. Mom
6. fix

Page 89
a jellyfish

Page 90
Answers will vary.